Reaching
Students

T0349509

In memory of my mother.

Reaching Students

Teachers' Ways of Knowing

Vivienne Collinson

CORWIN PRESS, INC.
A Sage Publications Company
Thousand Oaks, California

For information address:

Corwin Press, Inc.
2455 Teller Road
Thousand Oaks, California 91320
E-mail: order@corwin.sagepub.com

SAGE Publications Ltd.
6 Bonhill Street
London EC2A 4PU
United Kingdom

SAGE Publications India Pvt. Ltd.
M-32 Market
Greater Kailash I
New Delhi 110 048 India

Printed in the United States of America

Library of Congress Cataloging-in-Publication Data

Collinson, Vivienne, 1949-
    Reaching students: Teachers' ways of knowing / author, Vivienne Collinson.
        p.   cm.
    Includes bibliographical references and index.
    ISBN 0-8039-6227-4 (acid-free paper).—ISBN 0-8039-6228-2 (pbk.: acid-free paper)
    1. Elementary school teaching—United States.   2. Classroom management—United States.   3. Elementary school teachers—United States.   I. Title.
LB1555.C626   1996
372.11′02—dc20   95-50186

This book is printed on acid-free paper.

96 97 98 99   10 9 8 7 6 5 4 3 2 1

Corwin Press Production Editor: Astrid Virding
Corwin Press Typesetter: Andrea D. Swanson

Contents

Foreword

This book is about both teachers' and students' ways of knowing. The book represents a major departure from the studies of teacher thinking and expertise that dominated the literature during the last decade. Those works placed emphasis on teacher professional knowledge: knowledge of subject matter, curriculum, and pedagogy. Vivienne Collinson does not dismiss the importance of teacher professional knowledge. However, she directs our attention to the fact that this is only one form of knowledge. Professional knowledge may be a necessary condition for becoming a teacher, but in itself, it is not sufficient for becoming an exemplary teacher.

Collinson suggests that exemplary teachers develop a triad of knowledge: professional knowledge, interpersonal knowledge, and intrapersonal knowledge. These latter two "forms of knowledge" are two of the seven types of knowledge identified by Gardner (1983) in his "multiple intelligences" theory. Interpersonal knowledge is defined in terms of human relationships with students and with the educational and local communities. Intrapersonal knowledge is concerned with teachers' ethics, dispositions, and reflection. Exemplary teachers are teachers who have developed and integrated these three forms of knowledge. Exemplary teachers "learn to balance the three forms of knowledge" for the improvement of student learning (see Chapter 1, p. 10).

Six of the seven chapters start with vignettes that provide the reader with snapshots of exemplary teachers in action. What is particularly revealing about these vignettes is the focus on the teachers' ethics of care and concern as well as their commitment to teaching and to their students. What is noticeably absent from these vignettes is an emphasis on specific content mastery or on narrowly defined teacher expertise. The human side of teaching is highlighted. In each vignette, we see the personal qualities of teachers whose interpersonal and intrapersonal knowledge set them apart from adequate teachers.

The structure of the chapters gradually reveals the ecology of exemplary teachers' classrooms. After providing a conceptual model of becoming an exemplary teacher, Collinson takes the reader through the structuring and restructuring of the physical, social, and interpersonal environments of the classroom. As part of this restructuring, she introduces the concept of parents and professionals as "co-teachers." Collinson then comes to the heart of her book when she discusses structuring the environment for the development of ethics and dispositions. Each of these "structurings" gives us an "indication of how a teacher thinks about teaching and learning and what a teacher knows about a particular group of children" (see Chapter 2, p. 28).

Unlike other studies of expert teachers, Collinson focuses our attention on the structuring of the intellectual environment only after she has shared with us what constitutes teachers' interpersonal and intrapersonal knowledge. She does not make this choice lightly. All other structuring needs to be accomplished first or in interaction with the structuring of the intellectual environment. Collinson is very explicit about the unfolding of her ideas when she writes, "I have tried throughout the book to illustrate how these ethics can be modeled" (see Chapter 5, p. 65). Central to her argument is that the development of dispositions and ethics plays an important role in teaching and education because teaching reflects teachers' attitudes, sensibilities, and beliefs.

The structuring of the intellectual environment results in a type of constructive classroom. In this classroom, "the teacher does not try to model what to think but, rather, how to think" (see Chapter 6, p. 91). Children's ideas are respected. Children are encouraged to take risks, think deeply, and develop a sense that they can figure things out. This structuring of the intellectual environment promotes autonomy, creativity, and innovation in children's thinking and ways of acting.

Reaching Students: Teachers' Ways of Knowing is a wonderful book about teacher development. The concept of teacher development in most contexts is defined in terms of teacher professional development, which implies an increase in the teacher's professional knowledge. Teacher development in this book implies a way of being and becoming. Teacher development is a type of the highest form of adult psychological development. Exemplary teachers are "reflective, capable of understanding the assumptions, beliefs, and values behind choices and decisions." Collinson speaks of her teachers as having "learned to appreciate . . . multiple perspectives and the interdependency of relationships" (see Chapter 1, p. 15). She further describes exemplary teachers as "understanding that knowledge may be contradictory and incomplete." Exemplary teachers are able to "live with ambiguity" (see Chapter 5, p. 82). These characteristics of exemplary teachers have been described variously in the adult cognitive development literature as ways of thinking associated with the most mature forms of adult thought or, more simply, as "wisdom."

At the heart of this work is Collinson's observation that "for them (the students) to do better, I had to show them what 'better' looked like and then help them figure out what made the difference and how to improve their own work" (see Chapter 5, p. 78). Throughout this book, we get many glimpses of what "better" looks like through the eyes of exemplary teachers.

The audience for this book includes anyone who is concerned about the quality and improvement of teaching and, ultimately, of our schools. Collinson's writing, her examples, and the many quotations from exemplary teachers make this book accessible to all who care about the type of teaching that ought to occur in schools. This book should be required reading for all teachers in preparation and for their supervisors. A paraphrase of Collinson's own words applies here: If teachers are to become better, they need to see what better looks like.

Professional teachers will benefit from spending time in the company of exemplary teachers. This book provides professional teachers the opportunity to reflect on the attitudes, ethics, and dispositions of exemplary teachers. This reflection can function as a template for evaluating their own personal growth and development toward becoming exemplary. One of the most powerful images offered for reflection is the image of the teacher as learner, engaging students in ways of "figuring out" what they collectively know.

Vivienne Collinson's own background as a classroom teacher, resource leader, and now, professor and researcher represents the very combination of experiences and insights that suggests that she not only recognizes exemplary teachers but that she herself must be an exemplary teacher. Through all the pages of her book, she shows us "what better looks like."

Patricia Kennedy Arlin, Ph.D.
Professor and Head,
Department of Educational Psychology and Special Education,
University of British Columbia, Vancouver

Acknowledgments

This book benefited from the helpful suggestions of Rebecca Bible (early childhood coordinator, Columbus Public Schools, Ohio), Marilyn Dickson (executive assistant, Federation of Women Teachers' Associations of Ontario, Toronto), Felicity Finn (author, Wellesley, Ontario), and Anne Sylvan (early childhood coordinator, Columbus Public Schools, Ohio). I am also grateful to the researchers whose work in various disciplines has influenced my thinking, although they may not entirely share my perspective. Above all, I am indebted to the many exemplary teachers (professional teachers and parents) whose teaching, thinking, and wisdom provide the examples for this book.

CORWIN
PRESS

The Corwin Press logo—a raven striding across an open book—represents the happy union of courage and learning. We are a professional-level
publisher of books and journals for K-12 educators, and we are committed
to creating and providing resources that embody these qualities. Corwin's
motto is "Success for All Learners."

About the Author

Vivienne Collinson is Assistant Professor in the Department of Education Policy, Planning and Administration at the University of Maryland, College Park. She earned her doctoral degree in education policy and leadership at the Ohio State University and was the first recipient of the Outstanding Doctoral Dissertation Award from Delta Kappa Gamma Society International. She received certification in teaching and administration from the Province of Ontario and also holds administrator certification for the State of Maryland. Prior to her appointment at the University of Maryland, she worked as a classroom teacher for 20 years, a provincial resource leader in Ontario, and an Instructor and Visiting Assistant Professor of Education at the University of Windsor.

Collinson is the author of *Teachers as Learners: Exemplary Teachers' Perceptions of Personal and Professional Renewal* (1994). She has delivered numerous keynote addresses and presented many workshops on a variety of topics in both the United States and Canada.

Introduction

Why write a book about exemplary teachers? The use of the term—whether we use *exemplary, excellent, outstanding,* or any other similar term—is enough to threaten the strong egalitarian tradition among teachers, spawn nervousness that some teachers might be "better" than others, and raise the specter of competition in the form of merit pay and career ladders. In academic circles, the use of these terms can engender instant opposition and accusations of "elitism."

For a long time, we have heard the rhetoric about striving for and achieving excellence in our nation's schools. School districts continue to push for ever higher test scores while teachers urge students to try harder and to do better. My students taught me that they could not "do better" until they saw and learned what "better" looks like. Their insight made me wonder how teachers can become excellent if they don't know what excellence is or how it looks in classrooms. Not everyone has enjoyed excellent teachers during their school experience; not every preservice teacher has seen what teaching excellence can be; and not all teachers have had opportunities to observe or team teach with exemplary partners during their careers. Instead, isolationism (through choice, habit, physical struc-ture, or organizational structure) continues to be a pervasive feature of teaching, and prevents teachers from seeing what "exemplary" can be.

Thinking about educational and human excellence provoked three questions that provided the framework for this book: What is an exemplary teacher? What does excellence look like in the classroom? What do exemplary teachers do to reach students to help them learn? To help readers think about answers to these questions, the book offers a model for becoming an exemplary teacher, illustrates excellence in practice, and explains how and why exemplary teachers go to extraordinary lengths to know and reach students.

This book is about teaching and learning in elementary schools. There are many configurations of elementary schools, but for the purpose of this book, elementary schools are defined as kindergarten through 6th grade; in other words, children aged approximately 5 through 12. To offer a model for becoming an exemplary teacher and to illustrate how excellence can look in practice, I drew from the literature of various disciplines, classroom teaching experience, observations, conversations with teachers and parents, and research data. The results represent a beginning, not an end; an incomplete portrait, not an exhaustive treatment of this topic.

I wanted to write this book as a tribute to the exemplary teachers in our profession who make learning for children and themselves a top priority in their lives. I also wanted to write it to encourage beginning teachers to undertake the journey toward becoming an exemplary teacher. Educators do not expect novice teachers to demonstrate the smooth skills, wisdom, and knowledge of teachers who have spent—and continue to spend—time and energy on becoming exemplary teachers. So for beginning teachers, this book can be a point of departure. For all teachers, it can be a catalyst to encourage thinking, discussion, and ultimately, action. For administrators, it can provide ideas for changing practices to help children and teachers learn. For parents, it can underscore the importance of parents as students' long-term teachers and the necessity of working with their children's classroom teachers. For policymakers, it can encourage recognition of the complexity of teaching and the influence and social contribution of teachers who strive for excellence. I believe that a comprehensive portrait of exemplary teachers and excellent teaching is foundational to addressing issues of evaluation of student and teacher performance, career-long professional development for teachers, and organizational changes designed to support excellence.

Chapters 1 through 6 begin with vignettes that illustrate the contents of the chapter. The vignettes are based on true stories; names and some details have been altered to maintain confidentiality. Quotations that are not referenced represent teachers' comments transcribed from taped interviews.

Chapter 1 proffers a conceptual model for becoming an exemplary teacher through the development of a triad of knowledge:

- Professional knowledge (subject matter, curricular, and pedagogical knowledge)
- Interpersonal knowledge (human relationships with students, the educational community, and the local community)
- Intrapersonal knowledge (reflection, ethics, and dispositions)

The remainder of the chapter elaborates this proposed triad of knowledge; explains how these forms of knowledge work together to influence how exemplary teachers structure the physical, social, and intellectual environments in their classrooms; and briefly summarizes what we know about exemplary teachers and the importance of knowing students.

Chapter 2 indicates how exemplary teachers structure the physical environment of the classroom in ways that allow teachers to get to know students to help them learn. Teachers' considerations go far beyond organizing a smooth traffic flow to include observing cultural variations, using information technology, paying attention to student transitions, and preferring an organizational structure that may be one of the best-kept secrets of getting to know students: teachers keeping the same students for at least 2 consecutive years.

Chapter 3 discusses how interpersonal knowledge becomes the focus for creating an environment that encourages social learning, respect, and trust. Discipline in these classrooms is founded on respect. Trust is earned so that a collaborative culture fostering intellectual growth can result. Teachers pay attention to finding student strengths, encouraging them to take risks, and easing transitions for children. Interpersonal knowledge is also the focus of Chapter 4, concentrating on teacher interactions with parents via phone calls, home visits, and parent-teacher conferences. Exemplary teachers have reciprocal relationships with parents: They learn from parents, and they create ways to involve parents in children's learning at school.

Chapter 5 limits the discussion of intrapersonal knowledge to a description of how reflection, ethics, and dispositions shape the lives of exemplary teachers and influence the decisions they make in the classroom.

Becoming an exemplary teacher is closely tied to developing self-understanding, a disposition toward continuous learning, an ethic of care, a work ethic, and increasingly refined judgment. Teachers' descriptions help us understand how powerfully dispositions and ethics shape the classroom and influence teaching and learning.

Chapter 6 illustrates how exemplary teachers use professional, interpersonal, and intrapersonal knowledge to structure the intellectual environment in the classroom. These teachers emphasize conceptual understanding, learning to think well, and learning about learning. They work to set up dialogical patterns of listening and speaking in the classroom and indicate how observation, judgment, and criticism are vital to improving teaching and learning.

Finally, Chapter 7 proposes that the journey toward becoming an exemplary teacher involves a way of thinking and a way of being that reflects high levels of development in all three forms of knowledge: professional, interpersonal, and intrapersonal knowledge. Exemplary teachers continue to extend their own development to reach students. Knowing students and reaching students not only opens the door to better teaching and learning, it invites the rewarding possibility of contributing to the quality of life of other human beings.

Becoming an Exemplary Teacher
A Conceptual Model

Let such teach others who themselves excel.
Alexander Pope, 1711/1968, p. 681

Vignette: Creating a Web

Twenty-eight 3rd-grade students, their regular teacher, and their student teacher sat cross-legged on the floor in a circle. Models of whimsical insects (all biologically correct but made of household materials) floated overhead or graced every available surface in the classroom. The bulletin boards, painstakingly decorated by the children, were covered with students' insect stories, art, and musical compositions. As the class settled expectantly, there was a knock at the open door and a parent appeared, holding a spider made of a plastic bleach container, a tin can, paper drinking straws, and the hair of various troll dolls sacrificed for the sake of this project.

"Rachel couldn't manage this on the bus," the parent explained and winked as she handed the spider to the grinning teacher. "By the way, I have an insect cake we made for the class too. I'll get it from the car for you. Do you want me to put it in the staff lounge until you're ready for it?"

The teacher graciously thanked the parent and Rachel, noting that the insect cake was a perfect way to end the last day of the insect and spider theme and asking the class to join her in a round of applause. There was an immediate hum of discussion as the class discussed both the treat and the spider. Several children stood to help the student teacher hang the model on strings and hooks dangling from the ceiling while the classroom teacher stepped into the hall to chat with the parent.

When the teacher reentered the room several minutes later, she saw the beginning of a yarn web being formed on the floor. As each child received the ball of yarn, they gave a "spider or insect fact" to the class before rolling the yarn across the circle to a student who had not yet had a turn. The concentration was intense as the children not only recalled facts already given but made sure they did not repeat the same information. As the web of yarn grew more complex, the waits became longer and the excitement grew. Occasionally, a child would visibly associate a peer with a given fact and mentally search for something new to offer. At other times, a student would sit bolt upright, smiling hugely and whispering loudly to the teacher, "I know one we haven't said!" The tension was palpable as the ball of yarn was rolled across the floor to the last student, whose brow furrowed with intense concentration. Minutes went by as the class waited with anticipation. One little girl bounced in every direction, carefully avoiding touching the web, trying in vain to contain her excitement as her eyes danced.

"Can I please give Damion a clue?" she asked and promptly did so without waiting for the teacher's permission. The recipient of the clue glowed as he gave the last fact and the class erupted in cheers. As the noise subsided, the children looked expectantly at their teacher.

"Your web is beautiful," she said softly as she looked from the intricate pattern on the floor to the children's faces, "and you worked very, very hard. I would say such good thinking calls for an insect cake, wouldn't you? Rachel, would you please help Mr. Wilkinson get the cake while we figure out how we are going to organize the details so we can all enjoy it."

A Triad of Knowledge

As America struggles with growing public dissatisfaction with the education system and its increasing costs, we need to examine what excellent teachers are doing successfully to help their students learn. Much of the recent research on the professional development of teachers (e.g., Howey, 1985; Joyce & Showers, 1988; McNergney, Lloyd, Mintz, &

Moore, 1988) and proposals for restructuring schools (see Murphy, 1991) have improvement of teaching and learning as a fundamental goal.

Professional Knowledge

Shulman (1986) suggested that for this goal to be realized, teachers should be knowledgeable about subject matter, curriculum, and pedagogy. Such professional knowledge seems fundamental to good teaching; indeed, it has long been the core curriculum of teachers colleges. Because of this focus on professional knowledge for beginning teachers (e.g., Reynolds, 1989) and the traditionally strong emphasis on the technical or "how to" aspects of teaching in in-service workshops for certified teachers, it is easy to be lulled into thinking that professional knowledge will produce excellent teachers.

The professionalization of teaching has become a major reform effort of the last decade, set in motion by the Carnegie Task Force on Teaching as a Profession (1986) and the Holmes Group (1986). The leading advocate, the Holmes Group, includes the colleges of education of many leading research universities that endorse professionalization through expert knowledge, expanded teacher roles, and collegial interaction (Holmes Group, 1986); the creation of professional development schools with yearlong internships for beginning teachers and close collaboration between universities and these schools (Holmes Group, 1990); and major changes in today's colleges of education (Holmes Group, 1995). The concept of professionalizing teaching has come under scrutiny and criticism (e.g., Johnson, 1987; Malen, 1993), particularly the vision advanced by the Holmes Group (e.g., Labaree, 1995).

My experiences as a teacher, field supervisor, teacher educator, and researcher have convinced me that although universities and colleges can be very capable in building a solid foundation of professional knowledge, they have not focused on two other forms of knowledge: interpersonal knowledge and intrapersonal knowledge. Howard Gardner's (1983) theory of multiple intelligences referred to interpersonal and intrapersonal knowledge as two of the seven intelligences he has identified. He suggested that interpersonal and intrapersonal intelligence can be developed in individuals. I contend that developing this triad of knowledge—professional, interpersonal, and intrapersonal knowledge—is necessary for becoming an exemplary teacher and that we can learn about this triad of knowledge from those who excel at teaching.

TABLE 1.1 A Triad of Knowledge for Becoming an Exemplary Teacher

---

Professional Knowledge
  Subject matter knowledge
  Curricular knowledge
  Pedagogical knowledge

Interpersonal Knowledge
  Human relationships with students
  Educational community
  Local community

Intrapersonal Knowledge
  Ethics
  Dispositions
  Reflection

For the purpose of this book, I will limit the discussion of interpersonal knowledge to human relationships between teachers and students, teachers and the educational community, and teachers and the local community, particularly the parents of students. Similarly, I will limit intrapersonal knowledge to a discussion of reflection, dispositions, and ethics that teachers have discussed with me informally or formally. Table 1.1 elaborates the three forms of knowledge that I am convinced are necessary for exemplary teaching. I suggest that development of this triad of knowledge helps exemplary teachers structure the intellectual, physical, and social environment of the classroom, interact with other adults who know or work with their students, and benefit from extracurricular contacts with students to help them learn in the best possible ways.

Interpersonal and Intrapersonal Knowledge

We know that interpersonal knowledge and intrapersonal knowledge, especially in the form of self-understanding and reflective analysis, are vital to teachers' learning and self-renewal throughout their careers (Collinson, 1994; Reiman & Thies-Sprinthall, in press). Learning about these forms of knowledge is a career-long developmental process for teachers and there may well be many setbacks along the way. Some teachers are stronger in one form of knowledge than in another. But as the literature and examples in this book will make clear, exemplary teachers are those who have learned a great deal about professional, interpersonal, and intrapersonal knowledge so they can concentrate on their primary goal: helping children learn.

For decades, teachers have consistently reported that their chief reward is the knowledge that the children they teach are learning (Cohn, 1992). In other words, teachers enjoy "reaching" students and feeling that they have made a difference in at least some of the lives they have touched (Lortie, 1975). This strong motivation prompted one young teacher to return to teaching after leaving the classroom for a business career. She explained her reasons for rejoining the profession:

> I missed the altruistic mission of caring about American youth: teaching them valuable knowledge, skills, and competencies; preparing them for work; and helping them find meaning in life. I missed the collaboration and interdependence.

This teacher suggests that satisfying teaching goes far beyond reading, writing, and arithmetic to include the realm of human relationships. Interpersonal knowledge is not often emphasized in preservice teacher preparation programs or staff development agendas for practicing teachers, although recent literature points out its necessity:

> [Teachers] must cultivate and support human relationships: with other teachers, with students, with administrators, and with community. . . . Cultivation and support of human relationships . . . are the actions of teachers who embed their decisions in caring, and they are the actions of teachers who reach out to each other as colleagues, offering support and encouragement. (Bolin, 1987, p. 219)

Teachers' knowledge of their students and other adults, let alone the connection between this knowledge and caring and good teaching, is "only rarely an explicitly stated objective of formal education, although it is a frequently recognized and valued by-product" (Berscheid, 1985, p. 61).

This book underscores the human dimension by addressing:

- human relationships, caring, and excellent teaching;

TABLE 1.2 Communities Beyond the Classroom

Educational Community
  Colleagues (teachers, administrators, teacher educators)
  Professional organizations

Local Community
  Parents
  Taxpayers
  Interagency personnel

- strategies and resources teachers use in their efforts to know about students and whether they are reaching students;
- dispositions and ethics teachers model;
- teacher interactions with students and parents for the purpose of helping children learn.

Because exemplary teaching is a holistic, complex web of thinking, learning, and relationships, separating the act of teaching from interactions with students, the educational community, and the local community is difficult. Teaching in a neutral way that divorces teaching from the teacher's dispositions and ethics is impossible. So even though this book does not concentrate on professional knowledge per se (i.e., the specifics of subject matter and curriculum) or on teacher relationships within the educational community, the reader will notice throughout the book that when teachers discuss interpersonal and intrapersonal knowledge, they routinely refer to professional knowledge and to their peers. In their world, the African adage, "it takes a whole village to raise a child," is put into regular practice. They learn to balance the three forms of knowledge (professional, interpersonal, and intrapersonal) to support exemplary teaching and improve student learning. They interact with students, the educational community, and the local community to accomplish their goals (see Table 1.2).

I examined how exemplary teachers build and learn from human relationships with the educational community as a whole in an earlier book (Collinson, 1994). For example, exemplary teachers expand their scope of professional knowledge and involvement beyond the school to the national or international level, and they learn how to work within the political system of the district (also see Sternberg & Horvath, 1995). Relationships within the educational community are very important to teachers' development and need to be remembered in the equation of good teaching but are not a focus of this book. Instead, the focus here will be on relationships between teachers and students and between teachers and parents.

What Do We Know About Knowing Students?

When we think of "ways of knowing," the names of Gilligan (1982), Eisner (1985), or Belenky, Clinchy, Goldberg, and Tarule (1986) might quickly come to mind. The cornerstones of ways of knowing are questions about knowledge—questions such as "What do we know?" and "How do we know it?" These authors have helped us understand that there are many ways of knowing and many kinds of experiences that contribute to one's knowledge. The literature (see Collinson, 1994) indicates that exemplary teachers' ways of knowing may provide a wealth of insight into one area that these teachers perceive to be vital to excellent teaching: knowing students and knowing how to merge professional knowledge and personal relationships to reach students and help them learn. If this way of knowing is one of the keys to successful teaching and learning, it has implications for teacher preparation, teacher development programs, and the structuring of schools (including schools of education) so that teachers and students come to know each other well.

In a return to Dewey's (1933/1960) vision of schooling, some under-graduate and graduate programs are educating teachers to model "good habits of thinking." Good habits of thinking demand intellectual activities such as inquiry and reflection that lead to increasingly good reasoning and judgment (see Green, 1971; Rental, 1991; Schön, 1987; Simmons & Schuette, 1988). Also included in Dewey's vision is the idea of linking students' learning inside the school with what they have learned outside the school. Although the idea is far from new, we are seeing a resurgence of interest in building on students' backgrounds or prior knowledge, thanks to research in cognitive science (e.g., Resnick & Klopfer, 1989) and school reform (O'Neil, 1992).

Linking the curriculum with the students' worlds to show children the relevance of what they are learning in school is made much easier when teachers know the students and their worlds. But teachers' knowledge of their students and the strategies they use to acquire such knowledge are rarely emphasized in the literature as critical contributors to good teaching or as helpful to successful student learning. Yet whenever I ask teachers to talk about teaching and learning, they underscore the need to know students well in order to teach them well. Excellent teachers I have had the privilege to work with have an unshakable faith in their ability to make a difference in students' learning, and they go to extraordinary lengths to get to know students and parents in order to influence learning. They put the relationship between teacher and student at the heart of effective teaching, although by no means in isolation from relationships with other adults in their students' lives. The teachers' comments inspire several questions: How do teachers get to know students? How do teachers know they are reaching students? How do teachers use their interpersonal knowledge to help children learn?

The relationship between knowing others and good teaching has been discussed in the literature but does not seem to be a major focus or practice in preservice education programs, possibly because this knowledge is generally acquired over a long period of time and through a variety of experiences and circumstances. Preparation programs tend to focus on subject matter methods and "survival skills" for the classroom. Yet Willie and Howey (1980) noted "the need to understand the interaction of physiological, psychological, and social aspects in human development and the impact of that interaction upon one's self and the people one serves" (p. 27). They suspected that "the ability to experience open, supportive, even tender relationships not only with students but also with colleagues . . . is essential to good teaching" and that "reciprocity, self-disclosure, and mutual respect are essential ingredients in most authentic forms of teaching and learning" (p. 38).

One way the three forms of knowledge proposed in Table 1.1 merge is through the connection between the ethic of care and getting to know students. Berman (1987) suggested that teachers who are interested in caring do the following:

- come to know their students as individuals
- acknowledge that persons and things can be known both explicitly and implicitly
- create a classroom where people not only know but are known
- help students understand how knowledge is created and structured and used in the service of people
- establish dialogical patterns to involve listening and telling (pp. 207-208)

Heath (1980) also noted that teachers with a deep understanding of themselves and others (intrapersonal and interpersonal knowledge) "can analyze objectively, accurately understand, care for, and respect the diversity of their students" (p. 297).

What Do We Know About Exemplary Teachers?

Whether we describe exemplary teachers as *outstanding, expert, superior, excellent,* or with any similar term, they are clearly recognizable. Try asking someone to name at least one excellent teacher. Chances are they can describe that teacher in considerable detail. Chances are that somewhere in their description, they will talk about that teacher as a continuous learner, a caring person, and a committed teacher—attributes shared by exemplary teachers (see Collinson, 1994). The public can also tell you who among their teachers from kindergarten to graduate school was not a good teacher.

Jackson (1968/1990) noted that "although perfect agreement on who deserves the title may not exist, it is likely that in every school system there could be found at least a handful of teachers who would be called exemplary by almost any standard" (p. 115). My experience suggests that there is more than "a handful" of excellent teachers in many school districts; that colleagues, students, and parents can identify them; and that the identified teachers would be the first to say that *being* an exemplary teacher should more correctly be called *becoming* an exemplary teacher. For them, there is always more to learn, more to understand, new students to get to know, and different possibilities to try.

"Developing Teachers, Not Just Techniques"

The new national standards for beginning teachers describe some of the professional knowledge teachers should exhibit in the classroom, and although references to interpersonal and intrapersonal knowledge are made, the main emphasis is still on the professional knowledge necessary for good teaching. Several authors, however, have recognized the need for "developing teachers, not just techniques" (Heath, 1986; see also Bolin, 1987; Fullan & Hargreaves, 1992). Howey (1985) argued that one facet of teacher development should focus on understanding oneself and others. Heath

(1980), in his discussion of the psychological maturity of teachers, contended that teachers who have a deep understanding of themselves and others and who "can create collaborative working relationships with other teachers and their students will create more adaptive ways of teaching tomorrow" (p. 297).

Gardner (1963/1981) concurred, observing that self-renewing individuals (persons intensely interested in the process of lifelong learning) enjoy "mutually fruitful relations" with other human beings (p. 15). They are tolerant, loving, empathic, and dependable. "Love and friendship dissolve the rigidities of the isolated self, force new perspectives, alter judgments and keep in working order the emotional substratum on which all profound comprehension of human affairs must rest" (p. 16). As Westerhoff (1987) noted, "Teaching is a human relationship. It is the teacher as a person who is the key to learning" (p. 193). Because teaching depends on human interaction, excellent teachers must develop high levels of interpersonal knowledge.

Hunt (1971) and his associates recognized the importance of an interpersonal component in their conceptual systems theory and described it as how people conceptualize themselves, others, and the relationship between themselves and others (p. 18). "Higher conceptual level is associated with: 'lower stereotypy and greater flexibility in the face of complex and changing problem situation [sic], toward greater creativity, exploration behavior, [and] tolerance of stress.' . . . In interpersonal terms, the higher conceptual levels are associated with greater self-understanding and empathic awareness of others . . . creativity [and] flexibility" (p. 18). Stone's (1987) phenomenological study indicated that outstanding Teachers of the Year not only are creative, they also "genuinely love people and sincerely care about their needs" (pp. 136-137).

Sprinthall and Thies-Sprinthall (1983) confirmed that teachers at high levels of development exhibit dispositions of empathy and flexibility and high levels of humane and democratic values. Campbell (1988) also noted that in "expert" teachers, "continual striving for personal growth . . . was inextricably tied to a sense of humaneness and tolerance" (p. 50). Teachers who exhibit high levels of conceptual, ego, and moral development consistently perform better in complex situations than teachers with lower levels of development (see, for example, the synthesis of research in Glickman, Gordon, & Ross-Gordon, 1995 and Reiman & Thies-Sprinthall, in press). "The better people understand themselves, the less likely they are to be overwhelmed by events they cannot control . . . and uncontrollable events are a fact of life in the classroom" (Redl & Wattenberg, 1959, p. 494).

Leithwood (1990) and Reiman and Thies-Sprinthall (in press) have synthesized research on human development to describe teachers at the highest levels of professional expertise and psychological development. Such teachers are reflective, capable of understanding the assumptions, beliefs, and values behind choices and decisions. They have learned to appreciate multiple possibilities, multiple perspectives, and the interdependency of relationships. They are capable of synthesizing perspectives and of balancing the respective emphases given to students' intellectual achievements and interpersonal learning in the classroom. Excellent teachers use discipline effectively and control the classroom in collaboration with their students. They encourage complex functioning, learning, creativity, and flexibility to create intellectual, interactive classroom cultures.

Drawing on Interpersonal and Intrapersonal Knowledge

Knowing people is a prerequisite for interacting effectively with them (Berscheid, 1985). Knowing someone means learning their ethics and their dispositions (p. 67)—in short, how they think. Linking dispositions and thinking is not new (see Dewey, 1933/1960; Ennis, 1987; Jackson, 1987; Perkins, Jay, & Tishman, 1993). What is new are the attempts to understand how teachers' dispositions and ethics influence what they do in the classroom; in other words, why and how they make teaching decisions (e.g., Clark & Peterson, 1986).

The strong connection between dispositions and teaching and learning has not gone unnoticed (Collinson, 1994; Dewey, 1933/1960; Gardner, 1990; Howey & Strom, 1987; Katz & Raths, 1985). Although this book indicates that teachers do model or "teach" the dispositions and ethics they value, this facet of teaching is not well understood and has yet to influence education in a significant way. Tishman, Jay, and Perkins (1993) proposed that teaching "thinking dispositions" involves using an enculturation model of teaching that "emphasizes the full educational surround. . . . When teaching by enculturation, the tacit messages of the teachers' behavior, the physical space of the classroom, the tenor of classroom interactions, and the standards and expectations exhibited all become important" (p. 150-151). In a similar way, I will illustrate how exemplary teachers work toward creating a coherent and collaborative classroom culture that includes an intellectual, physical, and social structure designed to help children learn.

TABLE 1.3 Structuring Classroom/School Culture for Learning

Physical Structure
   Physical arrangement
   Organizational structure
   Routines

Social Structure
   Student roles and responsibilities
   Discipline
   Collaborative culture
   Encouragement to take risks
   Emphasis on students' strengths
   Climate of mutual trust

Intellectual Structure
   Variety in student grouping
   Students as teachers and learners
   Focus on thinking
   Emphasis on metacognition
   Teacher observations
   Multiple assessments
   Encouragement to question
   Time for reflection
   Interdisciplinary curriculum

Extracurricular contacts

I submit that what is generally referred to as professional knowledge is not sufficient to ensure exemplary teaching, although it plays a foundational role. I contend and will illustrate that professional knowledge is far more effective when it is balanced with interpersonal knowledge and intrapersonal knowledge within and beyond the classroom. This triad of knowledge appears to allow teachers to structure the intellectual, physical, and social environment in their classrooms in ways that increasingly improve learning for students.

Table 1.3 illustrates some of the ways teachers have tried to structure the classroom culture. This summary of issues teachers consider in structuring the physical, social, and intellectual environment of their classrooms is not meant to be exhaustive or conclusive. What Table 1.3 represents is what excellent teachers I have worked with as a colleague or researcher

TABLE 1.4 Ethics and Dispositions: Teaching for Life Beyond the Classroom

Ethics	*Dispositions*
An ethic of care	A disposition toward continuous learning
Caring/compassion	Curiosity/creativity
Respect for self and others	Risk taking
Understanding self and others	Problem finding and solving
Giving to and receiving from others	Responsibility
Courage	Flexibility
A work ethic	
Work ethic/pride of effort	
Dedication/perseverance	
Doing one's best	

consistently mention as important to them. The list is only a preliminary attempt to understand teachers' knowledge—knowledge that has been eclipsed in the past by an emphasis on the technical aspects of teaching in methods classes and in-service workshops.

There is one other facet of exemplary teaching that was mentioned earlier in the discussion of research-based literature but that is rarely discussed in the practical world of teachers, perhaps because we know so little about its effect in classrooms. This knowledge is part of teachers' intrapersonal knowledge and refers to their dispositions and ethics and to their capacity for reflection. "What we know about the best teachers is that they make it a priority in their lives to ask themselves continuously what they are doing and why, what builds meaning for them and others" (Zehm & Kottler, 1993, p. x).

I noted earlier that teaching is not a value-free activity, although some teachers take pains not to verbalize their preferences or values in the classroom. Nevertheless, teachers' ethics and dispositions influence the decisions they make regarding students, parents, and colleagues. My research indicates that exemplary teachers have sorted out certain dispositions and ethics that they believe contribute to a happy, productive life and that they "teach" or model these attributes (Collinson, 1994). Although not all teachers may be capable of articulating the ethics and dispositions they hold, I have met numerous teachers who can. This "in-between-the-lines" teaching (Collinson, 1994), or teaching for life beyond the classroom, is summarized in Table 1.4. Again, the list is not meant to be exhaustive; it merely reflects what teachers have reported to me.

Structuring Classroom Culture

Good teaching has become almost synonymous with methods classes because so much initial emphasis in teachers' preservice preparation programs is placed on the strategies or "how to" of teaching. Similarly, practicing teachers' "in-service education" or professional development has largely continued to emphasize the technology of teaching or new content to be taught. This is not at all to say that the technical aspect of teaching is unimportant; it simply has received most or all of the attention in teacher education. The assumption may be that little constructive learning can occur without good teaching techniques. Nevertheless, whenever I ask teachers to tell me about wonderful teachers they remember, they usually comment on far more than technique.

What appears to be the case is that excellent teaching represents a deliberate structuring of the physical, social, and intellectual culture in the classroom to provide coherent "enculturation" for student learning. In other words, teaching as illustrated in the opening vignette goes far beyond the use of a technique (the yarn web as a review or summative strategy) to include the following:

- Physical reminders of the thematic unit around the classroom
- Modeling of social niceties and ethics
- Opportunities for children to practice listening to peers
- Contribution to the profession as a *cooperating* teacher (a term used in many American districts to describe an experienced teacher who accepts a student teacher into the classroom as part of the preservice practice teaching component of the teacher education program)
- Human and public relations with parents-as-teachers

We have known for years that teaching the curriculum or "covering the course" does not necessarily lead to learning or understanding by students and that there is far more to teaching than meets the eye, particularly in the development of human relationships:

> For let no one be deceived, the important things that happen in the schools result from the interaction of personalities. Children and teachers are not disembodied intelligences, not instructing machines and learning machines, but whole human beings tied together in a complex maze of social interconnections. (Waller, 1965, p. 1)

Surely all parents and teachers would want children to be in classrooms where good teaching techniques are *de rigueur*. Teacher educators might argue that teaching methods must be in place if classroom management and human relationships are to occur. But to wish for teaching to be as straightforward as learning a "bag of tricks" or creating a repertoire of strategies is simplistic:

> Teachers may . . . at times wish for social distance from the complex, tangled, and sometimes destructive lives of their students, but they cannot both teach well and ignore the many dimensions of the lives of their students. Teaching well requires as broad and deep an understanding of the learner as possible, a concern for how what is taught relates to the life experience of the learner, and a willingness to engage the learner in the context of the learner's own intentions, interests, and desires. (Fenstermacher, 1990, p. 137)

What appears to happen in practice is that when new teachers begin their career, their efforts are concentrated on covering the curriculum and maintaining order. Even if they have taken human development, psychology, or sociology classes, the information may be momentarily forgotten or overlooked in the work, worry, and immediacy of the classroom during their first and second years of teaching. Although it would be naive to think that novice teachers could function in the same ways and at the same levels of development as exemplary veteran teachers, they could work on such development as part of their career development plan.

How interpersonal and intrapersonal knowledge complement professional knowledge to improve student learning (particularly through the physical, social, and intellectual structuring of classrooms) and how the three forms of knowledge overlap is the focus of the remainder of this book. The following chapters will illustrate how exemplary teachers synthesize and apply their professional, interpersonal, and intrapersonal knowledge to structure their classrooms, interact with students and the larger community, and teach beyond the defined curriculum.

Structuring the
Physical Environment

2

America's future walks through the doors of our schools every day.

Mary Jean LeTendre, 1955, p. 302

The August day was hot and humid and The Ritual had just begun. Each year for 22 years, Ray had taken a day off work to help LaWanda set up her classroom. She was changing grades and schools this year, and all of her personal furniture, books, and materials had come home for several weeks in the summer because of renovations at her new school. Neither LaWanda's husband nor their 11-year-old son, Jason, complained that the garage was off limits during that time. They knew that everything would go back to one of the district schools on a sticky August day. That day had finally come, and true to form, the temperature was over 90 degrees. LaWanda gave a last glance at her sheaf of notes and announced that everything was ready to go. The day would be long and hard.

LaWanda had organized the loading of the pickup truck so that the large items could be unloaded first. Off came a large braided rug she had found at a garage sale, followed by a comfortable sofa and a rocking chair. Next came a puppet theater, a water center, an aquarium, a terrarium, two bird cages, and a hibiscus tree. All were placed according to a floor plan LaWanda had made ahead of time to allow for quiet areas and maximum ease of movement in the classroom.

Ray and Jason left the school to buy sand for the sand center while LaWanda worked on the largest bulletin board. She had prepared the background at home—a school, a flag pole, and a playground. Now it only needed each student to attach a painting of themselves the first week of school. The day wore on and the heat intensified as each member of the family checked off the individual lists LaWanda had given them.

"I'll check with the custodian to see whether my flip chart and art easels have arrived," said LaWanda. "Jason, why don't you get the computers set up while Dad finishes the aquarium?"

Many hours later, dirty and disheveled, they looked around delightedly at a transformed classroom ready for a new group of first-grade students. Brightly colored plastic boxes held new crayons, sharpened pencils, glue bottles, and scissors on four round tables for eight. Large plastic crates under the water center held dozens of different shapes and sizes of containers that Jason had been assigned to collect during the past two months. There was a number line on the floor leading to shelves stocked with LaWanda's collection of children's books, music, games, Lego, felt cutouts, blocks, and puzzles. The refurbished puppet theater had a new velveteen curtain thanks to a sympathetic neighbor. Family and friends had been giving LaWanda hand puppets for years and Ray had built a gaily painted board with a hook for each puppet. The three paint easels were freshly stocked with baby food jars of paint and ingenious wire holders Ray had fastened on to the ledges so that wet paint brushes could drip into a replaceable tinfoil plate. Behind the easels was a bright bulletin board with various sizes of colorful paper picture frames awaiting children's masterpieces. Other frames already held art the incoming class had made in June with their kindergarten teacher. LaWanda wanted the children to feel comfortable and at home the minute they entered their new classroom.

"Time to turn off the computers," LaWanda said to Jason. "We're ready to go home."

"Do you have any idea how much money you've spent on this stuff?" asked Ray. "Do you think the taxpayers or trustees have any appreciation how much you subsidize your teaching, not just in actual dollars but in the time you spend going to garage sales and pet stores?" His grin took the bite out of his words, although LaWanda felt a twinge of guilt. She knew he was referring to their son's college fund.

"I don't know that the public appreciates it," she replied quietly, "but each year, my kids and their parents do. That's what's important to me. I wouldn't do it if I didn't think it made a difference."

Creating an Inviting Environment

"A primary responsibility of educators is that they not only be aware of the general principle of the shaping of actual experience by environing conditions, but that they also recognize in the concrete what surroundings are conducive to having experiences that lead to growth" (Dewey, 1938, p. 40). When babies are born, adults seem to know that they need stimulation. We hang mobiles above their cribs, use cheerful colors around them, and make funny faces or sounds to amuse them. As they grow, they continue to need stimulation, and while children's intellectual capacity grows, their physical surroundings remain important.

Teachers take a number of years to collect various items that act as teaching tools and stimulants in a classroom. Stores have a variety of bulletin board borders and other items that are reusable and that don't fade over time. Nevertheless, one observation I've made is that exemplary teachers have the children take as much responsibility as possible in the classroom. I've seen alphabet cards and games that the children, not the teacher, have created.

Some teachers swallow their pride and their desire for symmetry and neatness so that students can put up bulletin board displays. One teacher commented that when students have responsibility for at least part of their physical environment, they begin to recognize that they are active contributors to their learning instead of passive recipients of her teaching. Another teacher hung a large blank paper "quilt" on an uninviting wall and told the fifth-grade class they could fill each quilt patch with their art or photos as a memento of their year. A veteran teacher said that when parents of her students come into the classroom, "they smile at what they're seeing around the room. They're happy that their child is sitting in this pleasant place all day long."

Teachers know that the classroom environment, although apparently superficial, can be used to teach many lessons. Teachers often have all kinds of permanent teaching aids hanging around the room. But in one urban school where drugs were sold on the playing field after school, a fifth-grade teacher capitalized on every opportunity to teach her students, using even the physical environment:

You've got to have a place where the kids feel safe and it's got to be clean. I really bring that out to the kids, that when they see graffiti on our walls, they should be incensed that somebody did that to *their* school. I try to make it *their* school. It's *our* family here. Anything that happens here affects *everybody* and they should be really upset about graffiti and things broken on the playground. I think it's important that the whole community raises the child—the whole school community. So if the custodian sees them doing something, I want him to say something.

Exemplary teachers have learned to ask parents for help: Sometimes it's a simple request to send in tinfoil pie plates or baby food jars for the paint center; sometimes it's a request for volunteers to prepare something at home. For example, I've had parents work on props for drama productions or cut out shapes or pictures for specific lessons. When I taught first grade and wanted to incorporate a dress-up center into the classroom, a mother of five used items from her home and the entire neighborhood to provide the class with an astonishing center. We had everything from a clown costume to fire fighters' gear to a glittering fairy godmother's outfit. Later, she used her same contacts to organize a clothes closet at school for needy children who did not have adequate mittens, socks, boots, and the like.

Numerous teachers have plants, fish, or animals in the classroom, although sometimes children's allergies prevent this. One teacher explained her rationale for the environment she had created:

You have to make the classroom inviting and a learning experience. I try to pick unusual plants in my room—things that wouldn't necessarily be in a room. A lot of the kids have never had animals before in the classroom. And I know that it's an extra chore for me—dealing with fish, dealing with birds, dealing with all the other things that go with it. But on the other hand, I also know that caring for an animal brings about caring adults. I like to have my kids in charge, and after the first week of "I wouldn't clean up after this bird!" most of the children are begging me, "Can I go change the water now?" "Can I go change the feed now?" "Can I go scrub the cage down?" It's changed into a privilege! It isn't a chore; it becomes *their* pet. They really have a lot of respect for the birds. The first thing when the parents come into the room, they *have* to see the pets.

This teacher has learned to tap two areas of the human condition that rarely fail to evoke a positive reaction: first, that children respond to animals, and second, that almost any task can become a privilege depending on how it is handled by the teacher.

Teachers have figured out that rocking chairs have a soothing effect on some children and that certain textures invite stroking, which calms some children. I found out the latter by accident when I once wore a jacket with a velvet collar. As I checked a set of math questions, I realized that my student was absentmindedly stroking my collar as she struggled to think through an error. After that, I consciously tried to have a teddy bear and soft hand puppets somewhere near the reading area for younger students. Soft pillows or afghans are less obvious but equally effective for older students.

Teachers who use learning centers may do so for various reasons, but one teacher recognized the importance of variety and student options in the physical surroundings, especially for shy children who may not talk in a large class setting:

> I have a couch, a rug—private little corners and rugs that allow students to gather in small groups or be by themselves. Unless I'm doing a whole group presentation, I do my best with them many times when they're sitting on the floor or in a corner.

The same teacher also knows that in western cultures, physical height can be used to advantage as a deliberate tool of aggression or authority. Being at eye level with students is important to this teacher and others who sit on low chairs or kneel on the floor because they want to send a message of care, interest, and respect for equality in the classroom:

> I'll get them at their level. I'll sit down at their desks with a group of them. I'm not always towering over them. I'm a part of them at that moment.

Cultural Norms

Culture can also play a role in what so many of us take for granted. Most teachers who have student worktables instead of desks put communal supplies such as pencils, erasers, and scissors in the center of the table. But one teacher in a classroom that resembles a miniature United Nations discovered that her students have so little at home and deal with so much insecurity that they cannot share communal items at school. Putting the supplies on the table or on a shelf simply does not work:

> I know that a lot of people would argue with me that you should have community supplies. I find with so many inner city kids, they don't have anything of their own at home. Their [bed]room is not their own, they don't have a shelf for their things, they don't have crayons at home. They would much rather have *their* box of crayons and *their* pair of scissors and *their* pencil in their desk. "It's mine! Nobody's going to take it 'cause it's mine!" Every time I've tried with the "No, no, no. All the scissors go back into the box," they just take them and put them in their space anyway, or they hide them or steal them. And they *love* when they get books. The more books they get, the better they like it. Man, you can't get in their desk! They love having their own little space. I'm sure there's not enough trust and there's not enough feeling of having their own things at home. Now, I do have some children in the room who would have no problem with sharing. But there's still an awful lot who can't share.

Use of Information Technology

Information technology is one area that has affected all teachers' lives, but it has not necessarily had a huge impact on the physical or intellectual environment of every elementary classroom. However, one fifth-grade teacher in a science magnet school became very animated when telling me that she had just completed the most exciting year of her long career. Her grandchildren had originally piqued her curiosity about computers and she had spent several years becoming computer literate and knowledgeable about software and network possibilities. She volunteered her classroom for a special project that revolutionized the physical space (and how she teaches science!) thanks to the many networked computers in the room. As the students became accustomed to using technology for research and projects, she introduced them to the Internet as a way of finding out information to help them learn. They were delighted that other researchers, including university scientists, were willing to "talk" with them. Almost immediately, the teacher noticed that her students were preparing work at home and coming to school earlier and earlier to use their computers to get news and answers.

Knowing that a solar eclipse would soon be visible in the geographic area of the school, she used the eclipse as a science unit and had her students research where, why, and how solar and lunar eclipses occur. The students engaged in unprecedented levels of research, spending long hours at the computers and in discussion with each other as they prepared questions about the upcoming eclipse. When the teacher asked them why they were being so thorough, they said, "We need to sound very intelligent on the Internet when we ask *real* scientists our questions."

Organizational Structures

There is a particular organizational structure that is used only occasionally in schools but that may be one of the best-kept secrets of getting to know students: teachers keeping the same students for at least two consecutive years. I had my first experience of this nature in the late 1970s and loved it. For the first time, I realized how much time teachers waste on "review" in September, ostensibly to figure out our students' abilities and work habits or to ease them back into an academic environment.

The teachers I've met since then who have had the opportunity to keep children for consecutive years have also enjoyed the experience:

> I always enjoyed that, and I had one group three consecutive years. The development was astonishing. You really know the children and you know the families and the rapport is there, so you can start right out [in September] and do things.

Seeing the students' growth seems to be the most rewarding aspect for teachers:

> Oh, it's amazing! To go from kindergarten to first to second [grade], it's just *huge* jumps and leaps in their abilities. It really is a neat experience to have kids that length of time. People don't realize the jumps they make, especially in the primary grades.

For another teacher, knowing students and their families makes her role as teacher much easier:

I, too, have had that experience [of consecutive years with a class] and I think you really get to know a child and you really get to know the family when you have them for more than one year. And of course, there's the siblings that you've had before too. There's so much to be said for knowing people over time.

There is no doubt that teachers quickly establish a reputation in a school via the student grapevine. Perhaps hearing siblings and parents talk about teachers helps with the discipline part of that reputation, or perhaps there is some perverse quirk about human beings that makes children save their worst behavior for substitute teachers or teachers new to a school. Whatever the case, I noticed a very distinct decrease in discipline problems when I had students more than one year. I had long suspected that the key reason for their good behavior was that after the first month, they knew my expectations and I knew who to watch. Recently, however, another teacher gave me new insight into this phenomenon: I may not have had to discipline students because other children were doing it for me:

It really is a neat experience to have a class that length of time. They know my expectations and they help pass it on to the new students. If they see a student *not* doing something I'm going to be happy with, they'll say, "You better stop that. Mrs. Graham's going to get mad at you. She said you should do this and you *have* to do it." It really helps reinforce it and helps me do my job. I don't have to always say it. There'll be someone else saying it for me.

A number of teachers have worked with multi-age configurations where they may keep up to half of their class for a second or third year. They too have noticed how helpful "old" students can be:

It never stops—that good, conducive atmosphere where you think, "Oh, it's the end of May. We've finally arrived. We have this wonderful atmosphere with this little community of people." [In the fall], you still have the core of people that had been with you that year. It immediately helps. You don't have to get the new class started because that atmosphere is still ongoing. It just continues right on when you have that multi-age organization.

Another teacher believes that this organizational strategy helps both old and new students:

It takes away the anxiety of children because lots of times they
get a little apprehensive when they start the school year. "Who
will my teacher be? What will my teacher expect? Will I fit into
the structure of the classroom?" And the children who know where
they will be next year come in knowing the ground rules from the
start and they're ready to take off on an even keel. That makes the
new students' beginning smoother too because you already have
half of the population running just like they were [last year].

One exemplary teacher in a highly transient inner-city school asked
for this structure. She had discovered by accident that it was extremely
helpful for all of her students because structure and stability were the
factors most noticeably absent in their school career.

We've talked here about the importance of an inviting physical environment that is set up to do more than simply provide good traffic flow in
a classroom. The physical environment can also be used to get to know
students in order to help them learn. The physical structure of a classroom
gives an indication of how a teacher thinks about teaching and learning and
what a teacher knows or believes about a particular group of children.
Creating the physical surroundings for learning, however, is only the
beginning:

There's the physical environment of the furniture that lends itself
to learning, but it goes so far beyond that. It is the feeling that is
created. When you walk into various classrooms and buildings,
you get an immediate feel for the climate and that's what's so
important.

Classroom climate or culture has to do with the quality of human
relationships and interactions between the teacher and students as well as
among students. Exemplary teachers pay close attention to the nature of
social interactions and their impact on trust and learning. We turn our
attention now to teachers' interpersonal knowledge, which provides a
foundation for structuring the social environment of their classrooms.

Structuring Cultures for Social Learning

It is easier to be professional teachers than to share our lives as persons. To permit our life to be a resource for another's learning is to be vulnerable to compassion.
John H. Westerhoff (1987, p. 193)

Vignette: "Teacher, Please Don't Make Me Go Outside for Recess!"

A small hand tugged at Ellen's sweater as she scanned the children in the playground.

"Mrs. McPherson, Ginny's crying."

Ellen turned to follow the second-grade student who so urgently sought her help. Ginny was sobbing uncontrollably, near hysterics as her friend stared appealingly at Ellen. "There, there," Ellen soothed as she hugged Ginny and produced a tissue. "Tell me what happened."

"The kids said Ginny's pregnant," the little friend said solemnly. "That's mean, isn't it?"

Ellen felt pain tear through her heart as she looked quickly away. Like Ginny, she too had been a heavy child ridiculed with endless cruelty. She understood how merciless, how demeaning the comments had felt then, and how quickly the hurt returned now. Tears stung her eyes as she drew Ginny closer and said, "This isn't the first time, is it?" Ellen tried to explain to

29

Ginny that it was the inside of people that mattered, not the outside, and that her tormentors had been cruel. But she knew that her voice was only one among a chorus of society's voices extolling the body beautiful. She also knew that the old chant, "Sticks and stones can break my bones, but words can never hurt me" was very wrong. Jeering words uttered to a child could hurt for decades.

The following September, as the new third- and fourth-grade students filed into the open space pod, Ellen spotted Ginny. Throughout the year, Ellen noticed that Ginny either volunteered to help her teacher at recess or hid behind a book until the bell rang. Her refuge became a world of books where she could shut out other children. Ellen made up her mind. She would ask that Ginny be placed in her fourth grade come September and she would help her gain the social skills Ellen believed to be so vital to children's development.

That year, Ellen and Ginny's parents, with careful coaching, worked hard to convince Ginny to go outside every recess and to rise above the taunts. Ellen uncovered a highly intelligent child as she used every opportunity in the classroom to emphasize Ginny's strengths. In small groups, students began to get the message that Ginny was a valuable contributor to the group. At recess time, Ellen was at the door to make sure Ginny went outside to play. As Ellen monitored a steady and noticeable improvement in Ginny's social and intellectual world, she wondered what might have happened if Ginny had been allowed to withdraw into a world where she tried to cope with the pain by herself.

Eight years went by and Ellen heard snatches of conversation indicating that Ginny was doing well in school. Then one day, Ginny's picture appeared in the local newspaper under the caption, "High school women you should know." The next morning, as Ellen was writing the date on the board, a timid little voice said, "Are you Mrs. McPherson?"

"Yes, I am. How can I help you?" Ellen responded, startled that any student would be at school so early in the morning.

"I'm Ginny Amos' neighbor. Ginny says you might want to watch the 8:00 news this morning," the little boy said slowly and carefully, obviously trying hard to relay the rehearsed message correctly. The child smiled shyly as Ellen gave him her full attention, careful not to spoil the importance of the announcement. "Ginny's going to be on TV because she's a . . . she's a . . ."

"Quite a celebrity, I should think, to be appearing on TV," Ellen interjected smoothly and was rewarded with a toothless grin.

"I remember now," the child nodded with pleased satisfaction. "She said she's the featured guest because she's a volunteer at Children's Hospital. She said you'd know what that means."

Respect and Discipline

I've lost count of the number of teachers who have told me that one of their greatest pleasures and rewards occurs when former students write them notes or come back to visit them in later years. Teachers know that the child is not coming back because they remember specific lessons or facts, although they might do that too. What the letter or visit usually means is that the child has worked at improving social or nonacademic qualities somehow recognized as being valued by that teacher. These qualities are difficult to separate from some of the ethics and dispositions in Table 1.4, but they play a major role in how teachers structure the classroom and what teachers emphasize, if only through modeling. Recognition from a former student is a high honor and a form of appreciation that is treasured by teachers. Reciprocally, recognition (in the form of time or attention) from teachers is also treasured by students. Decades after the fact, one teacher still has the faded postcard her first-grade teacher sent her from Spain during summer holidays.

Closely tied to respect is the notion of discipline and responsibility. Veteran teachers will occasionally comment that discipline and responsibility are not what they used to be on the part of students or parents:

Sometimes I feel like I'm a missionary out there 'cause the hug kids get in my room may be the only hug they get during the day. You know, the pat on the back or my telling them I think they can be an author or a great politician or a great surgeon may be the only positive feedback they receive.

Lawsuits have made teachers wary of hugging or even touching children. I once had a second-grade student say smugly, "You can't touch *me*. My Dad will sue." But anyone who has taught primary grades knows that many young children regularly touch and hug teachers. And sometimes, as professionals, we swing the pendulum too far in the opposite direction, preferring zero physical contact instead of asking ourselves what might be appropriate kinds of contact in various circumstances.

Experienced teachers recognize that social development involving discipline and responsibility may be affected by a child's socioeconomic status or recent immigration to a new country:

> I think that with children who have such great needs as far as their family backgrounds, you can't worry about whether they're going to learn to read if they can't even learn what school is about and how you get along in a social setting. . . . You've got to start them off on the track of, "How do we get along just being in a room with 25 students and sharing with others?" While we're doing that, we're doing the stories and what-have-you, but I find that the social aspect for the children and for their mental health is *so* important: how to be a citizen and how to be a productive part of society. (Collinson, 1994, p. 77)

In a classroom such as the one described here, discipline and responsibility have to be altered to make sense in context. Nevertheless, when teachers talk about respecting students, part of their respect means that there are clearly explained expectations governing acceptable and unacceptable behavior in the classroom. The other part means that there is simply an unwavering belief that students are at school to learn and that the teacher's responsibility is to help that process along. Learning includes self-discipline and a responsibility to respect other students' right to learn at school. When teachers explain and model this line of thinking, older students tend to refer to them as "hard but fair." Even younger students appreciate honest communication, explanations for actions, and fairness. They also appreciate consequences that are clear, reasonable, and consistent:

> I'm very sincere and very real with the kids and my discipline is straightforward. I nurture kids when they need it, but if they're on my last nerve on purpose, they don't get much sympathy from me. I have a code of ethics in the room about how you act and how you don't act, and they know it. The only children that really misbehave in my room are the ones where it's beyond their control, medically speaking. That's not their fault, and it doesn't take the other kids long to figure that out.

The art of good discipline based on respect has to do with separating perceptions about the worth of the child from reactions to the child's act of misbehavior, a concept elementary school children have a very tough time understanding. When they misbehave, sometimes all it takes is "a teacher look" or the use of humor to deal with the problem, especially for minor infractions. As one teacher explained, "You've got to have a class that you can laugh and have fun with" and humor is a wonderful tool. Rather than reading the riot act to students on the first day of school, experienced teachers wait until an incident arises and then deal with it promptly.

One new teacher learned the important lesson of separating perceptions of the child from reactions to misbehavior by observing a veteran colleague known as caring, firm, and consistent:

> She knew how to be firm with the students yet not destroy their self-esteem. If she had a problem with a child, she dealt with it right then and there. She laid it on the line with that student and said, "You're either going to play by these rules or you're going to serve the consequences." But she did it in a way that the students listened to her and they respected her. I realized that by being firm with them, but in a caring way, the students responded very well and they found that you really cared enough to discipline them. I am in a very difficult school. The students are very demanding of your time and need caring and love.

Students can tell whether teachers are "mean" or sincere about caring enough to help children and about consistently taking the time and effort to discipline and follow through on consequences for misbehavior. One strategy that I found particularly effective in fourth grade and higher was to ask the students on the first day what goals they thought we could have to make our class a happy and safe place where we all could learn. If children have enjoyed disciplined primary classrooms, they know perfectly well by fourth grade what acceptable public behavior is. So once we had brainstormed a list of ideas, I asked them to figure out in the next day or two the five best goals they thought our class could work on throughout the year. We then came to consensus on the five goals we wanted and a student wrote them on large chart paper. "Our Goals" were hung at the back of the room so that if a student was being bothersome, I could simply ask the child to read the pertinent goal aloud. That usually was reminder enough to stop the misbehavior.

Also within the first week of school, the students came up with reasons why their goals were important to the class and to their learning. If the same student misbehaved a second time, I asked the child to refresh our memory about why the behavior was hurting his or her learning or the learning of others. The third part of the exercise to establish responsible discipline was for the class to help decide the consequences for misbehavior. This was not a random, free-for-all conversation. Instead, we had a serious discussion to evaluate the severity of disregarding a goal and to come up with the most fair and appropriate consequence for misbehavior. The children almost always chose consequences harder than I would have selected. On the rare occasions when my first and second reminders did not stop a misbehavior, I followed up with the agreed-on consequence and a phone call to the parent(s).

When beginning teachers think of discipline, they tend to envision it as a teacher-class scenario, perhaps because in teachers colleges, discipline must be discussed in the abstract and in general terms. However, exemplary teachers who appear to have "no discipline problems" or who are skilled enough to make teaching look easy know that a great deal of discipline occurs quietly with single individuals. Sometimes, proficient teachers are so observant and read body language so well that they can anticipate a child's move and physically, almost unobtrusively, position themselves close to the would-be perpetrator so that the action never occurs. Sometimes they may use a silent, light touch on the child's shoulder. They may also use private conversations with or suggestions for a child that can yield individual or group results, as illustrated by the following teacher's story:

> Danada was being a pistol; she has some abuse problems. But last week, we had a real tear-jerking episode where she was grabbing kids and heaving them in the air. I kept telling her, "Danada, that's not helping you have a friend, is it?" So yesterday and today, she was trying to stay near her space and stop going to their desks and kind of slamming things down. But Henry was bugging her on the carpet as we were reading a story. She got up, walked away from him, and came over and sat closer to me. I looked at her and said, "What happened?" And she said, "He was not bein' good, and you said to get away from people who aren't good. So I moved up by you."
>
> "That was *very* good!" I said. "I'm so glad you were smart. You didn't hit him or yell at him. You just walked away and that's the way to do it." [I was] complimenting Danada right in front of the group so that they see there are positive comments and "Oh,

she *did* do something good." They're more likely to try it next time if they know I feel happy about it.

A veteran third-grade teacher who uses terms of endearment with her students laughed uproariously as she described how a young student tested his humor and disciplinary limits at the same time:

> Kids don't miss much and one day, one of my little boys walked out of the room [the last student to leave at the end of the day] and said, "Bye, sweetie." I just laughed and out he went. He just wanted to play this game. There's a rapport, and he's going to listen to me and he's going to work. But if he gets out of hand the next day and I give him one of my evil eye looks, he's totally straightened out. So much is nonverbal. Kids need to learn what's appropriate and what isn't.

Teachers are generally aware that sometimes a cooling off period or "time out" is necessary for the teacher, the student, or both so that they can talk respectfully about a misdeed and why it was inappropriate. However, one teacher found out by accident that in addition to calling a time out, offering choices is also an invaluable asset in reducing power struggles when a student can't or won't accept respect and discipline from a teacher:

> One boy I remember was one of the nastiest young boys I'd ever seen. But if I got him away from the group and said to him, "You have a choice: You may either apologize to this person because you really hurt their feelings—and he would acknowledge he did—or you may go down to see the principal. The choice is yours. You have three minutes to decide." Invariably, he would decide to make the apology. But if you'd said, "I want you to apologize now," he would have stood on his head not to. If he were the one doing it, it was okay. If I made him do it, that was a horse of a different color, and you could not lead him anywhere that way.

This is not to suggest that a student can get away with an insincere apology or that sending students to the office is good practice. In fact, exemplary teachers rarely use the office and only as a final resort *if* the principal supports teachers and if students have learned that the office means the end of the road. What these stories are intended to illustrate is that there are ways to help children understand that respect and discipline are important to their learning and vital for getting along in social settings. However, knowing children well as unique individuals helps teachers understand how to read their nonverbal language to judge when and how to apply disciplinary measures.

Also worth noting is that most children have a finely developed sense of fairness and justice by the time they reach kindergarten. In front of a group, consistency is enormously important to the children and for the teacher's credibility. If there has to be flexibility within the rules, it is well worth the teacher's time to explain the rationale behind the alteration of the rule. Fortunately, there is much more flexibility disciplining an individual in private than in front of the class, and that may be why "hard but fair" teachers persevere to reach individual students. One veteran teacher said that the most important thing she did in her very first semester of teaching was to ask the class bully to wash her car for her. When she praised him for his fine work and realized his interest in cars, his classroom behavior changed completely; he couldn't do enough to help her. She had recognized the connection between knowing children and cultivating reciprocal respect.

Collaborative Classroom Cultures

Judith Warren Little (1982) has written extensively about collaborative cultures and generally discusses collaboration in terms of whole-school culture: "Without denying differences in individuals' skills, interests, commitment, curiosity, or persistence, the prevailing pattern of interactions and interpretations in each [school] building demonstrably creates certain possibilities and sets certain limits" (p. 338). This statement could just as easily refer to any classroom and the group of students making up that class. Dewey (1938) and Vygotsky (1978) both concluded that human interactions are important to learning. If we want learning to occur, it is in our best interests to make sure that human interactions help rather than hinder learning.

Elementary teachers may have more influence in creating a collaborative culture in their classrooms than the leader of a school might have. The teacher's advantage in helping to orchestrate and influence healthy human interactions is that elementary school children still see their teacher *in loco parentis*. Because of their youth, their habits of thinking and behavior are much less practiced than adolescents' and adults' habits and are, therefore, more malleable.

Each class tends to take on a personality of its own and some are much easier to deal with than others. Most veteran teachers have had a "dream class" or "the class from hell" at one time or another, and they know that their preferred structures for fostering productive student-student or student-teacher interactions have to be altered accordingly. Sometimes, both intellectual goals and social goals suffer, even when exemplary teachers make their best effort. One teacher agonized over the feeling that she was not able to do her best academic teaching one year because she could not structure the social interactions at the level she had come to expect from fourth-grade students:

> I think teachers know the problems and sometimes we know that we can't solve them. I had this one class that was horrendous and I had to be like the Gestapo. The next year, they went to fifth grade to a teacher who had come from a class of students who wanted to learn, were ready to learn, and were self-motivated. I went up to her and said, "With this group, you can't be this warm, loving person because it doesn't work with them. You've got to learn to deal with this particular class." I tried everything with them and I went home feeling like I was the wicked witch of the north every single day. I didn't feel like I succeeded with them. I didn't feel like I had accomplished anything. I just felt like I had kept them under control for a year.

More typically, however, teachers are able to make progress in structuring collaborative cultures so that they and their students can make intellectual development a reality. An exemplary teacher told me that one of her greatest classroom rewards from students is to hear the words, "I can't wait to . . ." To her, the words represent "the power of rereading and reliving things so that you can learn more or look at it in a different way. For students to get that is very satisfying." When I commented to another teacher that it seems as though the classroom environment and the personal relationship between teacher and student have to be secure before you get that kind of spontaneity from a student, she said,

> That rapport? Yes, I think too many times we get too involved with the pieces of the curriculum. To me, it is never a waste of

time to spend quality time building that rapport. That rapport you have, the atmosphere you've created in that classroom, is crucial.

Encouraging Risk Taking and Student Strengths

Exemplary teachers seem to work hard at two particular facets of collaborative culture. The first facet has to do with establishing the right of everyone in the classroom to make mistakes and learn from them. This may be explicitly stated but might also occur when the teacher makes a mistake, laughs, and says, "Boy! That sure didn't turn out the way I thought it would! How do you think I can fix it?"

> Students need to see teachers who admit that they make mistakes, and if you make a mistake, you say this is a learning experience. I always tease the kids and say that's why erasers were put on pencils: When your eraser's gone, just scratch out the mistake.

Students with perfectionist tendencies are worrisome because of the pressure they put on themselves (and sometimes on others) and also because they risk cutting themselves off from learning if they are afraid they'll make a mistake. As Tim McMahon (1995) remarked, "Risk-taking is inherently failure-prone" (p. 177). Learning how to deal with failure is an important part of learning, and teachers need to be attuned to how their students respond to mistakes and failures. Sometimes teachers have to be blunt with perfectionistic or fearful students and ask the students dozens of times to verbalize the worst possible thing that could happen if they make a mistake at whatever they are doing; typically, the reply is, "I don't want to look stupid." This technique of articulating the worst case scenario until it becomes a self-monitored practice is usually successful at countering an imaginary or overblown consequence of making mistakes. Sometimes, teachers reiterate the same idea in a different way:

> Nothing happens if you make a mistake. You learn from it and hopefully you won't make that same mistake again. But nobody is perfect and you never stop learning. I always say that to my kids. I'm an adult, but I'm still learning things. And I tell them that I learn from them as well. Every day you learn something new.

Students take a risk every time they raise their hand or try something new. Structuring a social environment that respects and honors students' risk taking is fundamental to learning:

> They must have an atmosphere where they can take risks. I tell my students straight out that we learn from our mistakes. If you know it's a mistake, you've learned that it's a mistake and you try something else. You create a [culture] where they know that we're solving problems together and we're not always going to get it right the first time. We don't all see things the same way, and sometimes children don't see things the way we see them [as adults]. So I look at it from their perspective and step back and say "What is this child doing?"

Students' mistakes in thinking are often logical when we look at situations from their perspective, given the information or misconceptions they may have. When information is not making sense to students, they need to feel free to say so:

> Sometimes children are very threatened if something's not sinking in and they'll freeze and not do much. But if you have the kind of atmosphere where they know that this is a learning experience and it's okay to say "I don't understand," then they will come up and ask you or ask someone else in the class. They need to know that we are a group and that they are free to talk to one another [to learn].

Exemplary teachers know their students well enough as individuals to recognize when a child is asking a serious question, is being too lazy to search for an answer, or simply needs some of the teacher's attention. When students ask a serious question, these teachers often say something like, "Hmm. That's a very tough problem. Who do you think we have in the class who could help us out with that?" This response underscores the second facet that seems critical to encouraging a collaborative culture: pointing out students' individual strengths. Finding strengths in some children takes longer than in others (especially if children are quiet and introverted), but excellent teachers persevere because they know the long-term benefits for each child are valuable. As one teacher explained,

> I think it's important for the teacher to point out strengths in children during the school year. Everyone is strong in something and children need to be built up so that no one feels that they are the child who's left out. Teachers need to find everyone's strength and really build it up so that the children feel that they are successful in whatever way possible. A child who may be having difficulty reading may be the world's best artist.

Children, especially in primary grades, learn quickly which peers excel in which areas and seem to enjoy the opportunity to help other students.

In my first school, one of the kindergarten teachers caused untold tragedy in her room because she did not pay attention to developing positive attitudes toward mistakes and because she did not concentrate on finding and recognizing children's strengths. Her kindergarten pupils discovered fairly early in the year that the teacher approved when they got perfect scores on their worksheets and rewarded them with colorful and much sought-after stickers. The class also figured out quickly that Bill got the most stickers. They arranged to have him sit behind a room divider and find their mistakes, which they then corrected before delivering their worksheets to the teacher. The teacher did not take long to find out why she suddenly had so many beaming faces admiring her rapidly dwindling supply of stickers. The situation was handled insensitively and negatively with Bill and his parents. Although five-year-old students cannot legally "drop out" of school, Bill began to hate school and mentally dropped out for a year before a kind teacher recognized his intellectual ability. The class realized with deep sadness that they had somehow contributed to Bill's being in trouble and did not understand how getting perfect scores on papers could make the teacher so angry when earlier it had seemed to make her happy.

Knowing Students: Creating Trust

Teachers can develop a sense of trust in students within the classroom by being fair, reasonable, respectful, and consistent. They can find opportunities to showcase students' strengths and discover their personal interests. There is something so special about teacher-student rapport on a personal level that when there is rapport on only an academic level, it makes teachers feel that they're missing out on a great deal of knowledge.

Empathic teachers find ways to invite trust without prying. Their motivation is to help the child in some way:

> I believe in being totally up front with students and I say things to them like, "If you want to write something to me in your journal that's hard to say or something that's private to share with me, feel free to do so," because they don't always know that that's okay.

Another teacher has a mailbox in the classroom for everyone and the class learns that letters are private.

> I've also made it very clear to my students that if there is something that they need to talk to me about privately, all they need to do is write me a little note or tell me and I'll have lunch in the classroom with a student or a group of students. Lots of times in my mailbox, I'll find notes that are of a personal nature. Somebody just needed someone to listen to them. So I think the students need to know that they are free to do that, and lots of kids won't say something verbally, but they will write it down.

This knowledge is not a one-way exchange. Using professional judgment, exemplary teachers share enough of their personal life to allow students to learn to know them as a teacher and an individual:

> I remember when I was in graduate school, I was shocked to find out that one of the least used languages with teachers and students is personal language—that teachers do not share their personal lives with their students. I never did that. My children in school know about my children at home, and they know about my background. They are always asking me questions about "What did you do over this vacation?" I try to mesh my personal life with my life at school so that they realize that I don't live at school, so that they know I'm a Mom and I'm a teacher and I have children and I have a husband and I was going to school, so that they know me more than just this lady that is in my room at school.

This teacher's comment mirrors that of psychologist Carl Rogers (1969): When teachers spend time and effort developing human relationships, they become "a *person,* not a faceless embodiment of a curricular requirement, or a sterile pipe through which knowledge is passed from one generation to the next" (p. 107).

Another way to share personal knowledge is by the judicious use of relevant stories or anecdotes:

> One sure-fire way to spice up a rather dull lesson, and some lessons are just kind of dull by nature, is to give a personal anecdote or tell a story. It also helps [students] associate that rather dull piece of information with what are you trying to get across. There'll be that link to help them remember.

Caine and Caine (cited in Pool & Willis, 1993) explained what this teacher has discovered:

> "We think with our feelings; we feel with our thoughts. . . . The brain is not divided into an emotional part and a learning part; it remembers facts best when they are embedded in experience, and it makes meaning best when it feels the meaning." (p. 2)

I remember being amused as a novice teacher when the parents of one of my students came to a parent-teacher conference and implored me to ask their son to clean up his bedroom. They had exhausted all rewards and punishments and were getting nowhere. I laughed and said that although I might be able to help their son academically, I couldn't see how my exhortation could help with the bedroom problem. They both looked at me in astonishment and said, "But Rob thinks you're next in line to God! If *you* tell him, he'll do anything." Rob had played our lead role in the annual musical and I had spent many hours coaching him. Thanks to his parents, I thought long and hard about the effects of teachers' attention on children inside and outside the classroom. There are no grades assigned to extracurricular events, so the relationship between the teacher and student is subtly altered and the atmosphere usually more relaxed. Just as the teacher sees the different strengths, abilities, and interests of the child through nonacademic contact, so the student begins to perceive the teacher differently. The results of those extracurricular exchanges can have very positive effects on children's learning and behavior in the classroom. This special kind of exchange provides a special kind of trust.

A similar sort of exchange can occur during conversations with students at recess or lunch time:

[Being on duty is an opportunity] to get to know the children because they talk in a more personal way when they're in a lunchroom or when they are on a playground, and they share little stories with you and tell you things about their backgrounds.

Being on duty is not one of the most sought-after activities in a teacher's life, but the contacts made while on duty may well have good (or bad) repercussions in the classroom:

If you've done some things in the lunchroom or outside with them, they're much more likely, once you're back in the classroom, to stay on that level of personal contact. You're not just that authority teacher figure. They see you in many roles.

Sharing who we are with others is a huge risk; being honest or "real" may make us vulnerable. Children have a wonderful capacity for recognizing honesty and respect, and unless too many adults have destroyed their trust, few children will turn away from adults who like them, respect them, and are trying to help them. Exemplary teachers seem to persist because they believe that informal knowledge of each other assists students' formal knowledge acquisition in the classroom.

Respecting Transitions

There is one other social aspect to which schools pay very little attention: transitions. Some schools have welcome kits of information for students entering the school part way through the year. Others use student partners to help newcomers adjust. Of course, teachers try to welcome their new class in the fall as warmly as they can. But we sometimes forget how difficult new faces and places are for us as adults, let alone for young children who can get very apprehensive about who their new teacher in the fall will be.

In open space schools with team teaching, children may have seen their new teacher ahead of time or they may stay with their team of teachers for several years. In schools using multi-age configurations or in which teachers have a class for consecutive years, children may also know their teacher and avoid tough transitions. In the Chapter 2 vignette, The Ritual, the teacher made sure her students' art was up so there would be something familiar when they entered their new room. There are other possibilities for allevi-ating children's apprehension that are also well worth the time:

> A lot of self-contained schools make sure that the students for next year have met their new teachers. They take time at the end of the year to introduce everybody. I've had students write letters to the new students coming in to make them feel welcome. So initially, that morning at the end of August when they walk in, there's a letter on their desk from somebody who sat there last year.

Whatever attempts teachers make to help children learn social skills that will help them in the present and in the future, there will always be something else that can smooth the way for students. Teachers who recognize the importance of knowing their students well continue to work at structuring cultures for social learning to support students' academic learning.

The teachers also draw on interpersonal knowledge through the edu-cational and local community. I mentioned earlier that exemplary teachers' search for and application of interpersonal knowledge is explored in the book, *Teachers as Learners: Exemplary Teachers' Perceptions of Per-sonal and Professional Renewal* (Collinson, 1994). The educational com-munity, for example, plays an important role in teachers' knowledge of how classroom teachers, administrators, teacher educators, and profes-sional organizations can work together to contribute to the improvement of teaching and learning. The next chapter will examine how the local community, especially students' parents, can play a vital role in providing classroom teachers with other ways of getting to know students.

Working With Parents

Our Students' Long-Term Teachers

4

One looks back with appreciation to the brilliant teachers,
but with gratitude to those who touch our human feelings.
Carl Jung (1954, p. 154)

Vignette: Schooling and Education Aren't Synonyms

Karen Douglas looked around her kindergarten room one last time before
her first appointment. She had fought for years to have the principal and
district approve a staggered entry for her classes so that she could meet
individually with each parent and child by appointment before the whole
class came together. She mailed an invitation to each family at the begin-
ning of August, requesting that they confirm or change their allotted time
for the meeting.

Accompanying the invitation was a short questionnaire for each new
student. Karen had been making small changes to the questionnaire for as
many years as she could remember whenever new experiences and parental
suggestions occurred. She was constantly surprised at the high number of
parents who filled it out ahead of time and remembered to bring it to the
meeting. "I guess I shouldn't be surprised," she confided to a colleague,
"but I have to keep reminding myself how important the first day of
kindergarten is. Sometimes it's more traumatic for the parent than for the
child."

There was a light tap at the door and Karen turned to greet the tall mother and fragile-looking child in the doorway.

"I'm Katrina Lenz and this is Christopher. Christopher, this is your new teacher, Mrs. Douglas." Winking at Karen, she added, "Our little neighbor, Ginger, plays school with Christopher and always pretends she's you. You certainly made a good impression on her two years ago."

Karen had toys, art supplies, and books near the table where she sat with the parent, and she always watched with interest which children would leave the protective circle of the parent and wander over to the toys. She smiled as Christopher left to explore them almost immediately.

"It'll be the Magic Markers," Mrs. Lenz predicted. "We know we're biased, but Christopher is a very good artist. I'm sure he'll have something to show you before we leave."

Twenty minutes later, as Karen drew the meeting to a close, Mrs. Lenz dropped her voice and said, "We'd like you to be aware of a difficult experience our family is having right now. My mother, Christopher's grandmother, is staying with us. The doctor has given her only one or two more months to live and we have tried to be as open about aging and death as possible with Christopher. But if he goes on about it in class or if his behavior changes, we'd really appreciate a call."

"I'm glad to know that," Karen said kindly, "and I very much appreciate what Christopher and your family must be going through. Thank you for helping me understand and thank you both for coming."

"Ready to go?" Mrs. Lenz asked Christopher, who did not hear her until the third call.

"I haven't finished yet," he finally said with annoyance.

Karen gasped as she looked at his paper. He had sketched the outline of the vase of flowers she had placed on the corner of her desk and was carefully shading the petals of a rose. Mrs. Lenz rolled her eyes heavenward with amusement and then knelt down to look her son in the eye. "Remember the new markers we bought yesterday? What do you think about using them to finish your picture at home and then giving your art to Mrs. Douglas when you come back on Friday?" Christopher wavered and then proudly announced to Karen that he now knew how to sign his art work. Karen grinned and told him she would put the sketch on her door for everyone to enjoy when he brought it back.

September came and went and Karen's class was looking forward with great excitement to their field trip to a pumpkin farm the following Monday.

Mrs. Lenz and several other parents had volunteered to accompany the class. On the Wednesday before the trip, Christopher was absent, and Ginger brought a note saying that Christopher's grandmother had died. Karen took a rose and a card to the Lenz house before school the next day and was surprised to hear Mrs. Lenz reassure her that she and Christopher would go on the field trip.

On Monday morning, Katrina Lenz wondered why Christopher did not come downstairs for breakfast when he was called. Tiptoeing upstairs, she was stunned to see Christopher still in his pajamas, swiping thick black strokes across a piece of paper. He never used black in his art. Looking more closely, she saw a small, detailed wooden casket untouched in the chaos of the black background.

"Are you feeling angry about Grandma?" she asked softly as she hugged him.

"I'm not going on any stupid field trip!" he shouted as his chin quivered.

"Honey, just because Grandma died doesn't mean that we can't love her or think of her or talk about her anymore. We have all kinds of videos and pictures with her that made us happy. Why don't I get the album of your last birthday with Grandma while you get dressed?"

Running downstairs, she grabbed the phone and dialed Mrs. Douglas.

"Christopher is having a really hard time this morning. I think I can talk him into going to school, but it looks like we're going to be late. We'll do our best."

Christopher climbed into his mother's lap with the photo album and curled up, slowly talking his way through the birthday photos. Glancing frantically at the clock, Katrina managed to say, "I just had a great idea! I bet Mrs. Douglas would love to have a new picture from you. What do you think?" Without a word, Christopher walked over to his little art table. Minutes ticked by as he concentrated on his picture.

"There!" he said at last. "I'll just show it to her today and then I'll put it on the fridge."

The picture was a delicate pastel of Christopher, his grandmother, her cats, and a rainbow. Katrina surreptitiously slid the first picture into her handbag. As they parked the car at the school, the kindergarten class was just beginning to board the bus for their trip.

"I'm so glad you're here," said Mrs. Douglas, hurrying over to meet them.

"This is for you," said Christopher, offering her his picture. "You can have it today, but my Mom's going to take it home with us."

"It's perfectly beautiful!" Karen said. "I'm so happy I can share it for one day."

Nodding, Christopher ran over to the bus. Katrina opened her handbag.

"This is why we were late," she said, showing Karen the first picture. There was a long silence as Karen read between the lines and realized that she was witnessing a very important, very private experience.

"Thank you," she said simply. "You have taught me a lot about compassion and patience and courage. I don't know how to thank you, but you've helped me be a better teacher."

Parents and Professionals as Co-Teachers

> Research on social development, attachment theory, and teaching and learning demonstrates the importance of adult-child relationships in children's development. . . . Child-parent relationships play a prominent role in the development of skills and competencies necessary for school success. . . . A child's relationship with an adult might be said to "organize" the child for learning and for social interaction. (Pianta, 1993, p. 1)

Schaps and Solomon (1990) also emphasized that caring, stable adult-child relationships are foundational for children's intellectual, social, and moral growth.

Children learn the divide-and-conquer survival strategy at a very young age, and experienced teachers know that they must get parents working with both the teacher and their child. One teacher had to be very explicit about this priority, yet make the parent understand that her motive was to help the child become responsible and independent. The teacher also wanted the student to learn that grades are earned by a student, not negotiated by a parent:

> I said to a parent one time, "Do you think Alexis is smart?" And of course the reply was positive. So I said, "Don't you think she's smart enough then to figure out that we're not working together? She doesn't have to do the work or study because she knows that as soon as I put a grade down here, you're going to come marching through the doorway."

Teaching is not limited to just teaching students. Being a teacher involves interacting with students' parents or guardians as well, although we have not emphasized working with parents as much in recent decades as we do today. Most schools where I worked were not very responsive to the many immigrants who did not speak English and were still suffering culture shock when they registered their child and met the teacher. A few political refugees had not ever had the opportunity to attend school; many newly arrived parents were not familiar with our school system or with Western expectations, curriculum, and assessment instruments.

We are doing more today. For example, I recently met a Chicago principal who is encouraging a teacher to share a written account of her attempts to understand and work more effectively with the two large ethnic groups in the school. But there are still schools that greet parents with versions of the commercially produced sign, "All visitors must report to the office immediately." For parents who are already uncomfortable coming to school, perhaps because of unhappy experiences in school, perhaps because of ethnic or language barriers, this authoritarian order does not suggest a warm welcome or conjure up positive images of school.

Despite some schools' failures to involve parents or treat them well, there have always been individual teachers who recognize that they are co-teachers with parents. Usually, parents or guardians know their children far better and in many more ways than teachers:

> When children go home from school, they're with somebody else until the next morning. So it's very important that parents understand that you need their cooperation because you can't do it alone.

Yet even though parents know how their children behave when they are at home, they don't necessarily know how children behave in a large group. I remember complimenting a parent on her son's politeness to others in the classroom. She was taken aback and said, "Sure wish some of it would rub off at home!"

Sometimes, circumstances do not permit a parent to come to the school, but teachers still try to find ways to communicate so that the parent can show interest and support at home:

> I've heard negative comments about parents, but my experience is that most of them really have the best interest of the child at

heart. Many times when they believe the child instead of you, it's just because they love that child so much, they think the child can do no wrong. If you can explain enough about what you're trying to do—at curriculum night and Open House, in conferences, letters, telephone calls—it helps a lot because they begin to trust you. This year, I've got a couple parents who don't get a chance to come, but most of them will respond in some way, maybe by returning a note, "I don't have time this year" or whatever. At least they took the time to respond. If kids see that Mom or Dad's interested, then they're going to do what they need to do for school.

This teacher reminds us that when parents send their young child to school after summer vacation, they may be entrusting that child with someone who is a total stranger.

Establishing a good reputation in a school can be very helpful. One teacher noticed at the beginning of school that a student was getting himself into difficulty by trying to be "Mr. Cool." At the first opportunity, the teacher described her observations to the parent and asked for help. She was happy to receive both parental support and the reason for it: "I have a friend whose children you taught and he thinks the world of you. He says I'm so lucky to have you as Jimmy's teacher."

Another teacher recognized that her efforts to work with parents have increased over her career and have been reciprocated:

There's always one or two who don't communicate back or you have a hard time reaching, but on the whole, it's been a wonderful experience. I didn't always do it to the extent that I do it now. I always knew it was important to have a good relationship with parents, but in the last few years, they have really made an effort to get to know me and I've worked hard to get to know them. People will call and say, "I saw this article that you'd be interested in" and will send things in. One parent who works at the art gallery always advises me about programs. And I try to do that for the parents too.

Sometimes this teacher consults with the child's previous teacher to find out how that teacher built up the parent-teacher relationship. Aware that many teachers will not give out their home phone number, this teacher does give her number to parents because she feels so strongly that "we need to do this together—the students, the teacher in the classroom, and the parents at home."

Communication is a two-way street and exemplary teachers work at finding ways to keep parents informed. One of the best ways to stay in weekly or monthly contact with parents is by using a calendar. Kindergarten teachers routinely send home classroom calendars to remind parents of field trips, provide the unit topics of study, or list library book exchange days. But no matter what the grade level, calendars are a useful tool for teachers and a welcome means of communication for many parents. Of course calendars are extra work for teachers, but they can also be advantageous. They help teachers to plan and organize at least a week ahead and they provide supportive evidence when parents accuse teachers of not informing them about homework or projects until the night before they're due. One teacher, having learned from experience, now laughingly explains to parents in September that if they do not see her weekly calendar for three or four weeks, they should be suspicious of any story their child has fabricated and call her. She has also learned that writing little anecdotal comments of praise or concern each week on individual students' calendars are appreciated by students and parents.

Going the Extra Mile to Learn From Parents

Meeting parents to create trust and establish a partnership to know and help students is so vital to exemplary teachers that they are not satisfied with the ubiquitous Meet The Teacher Night three or four weeks after school begins. The vignette at the beginning of this chapter describes how a kindergarten teacher structured individual meetings with each parent and student during the first week of school in the fall. This can be done effectively at any elementary grade level so that the child gets a clear message that there are communication lines between the school and home and that the lines are open because the teacher cares about the child. Usually, however, only kindergarten teachers have the luxury of scheduling meetings during the first week of school.

Telephone Calls or Meetings at School

Instead of trying to schedule meetings before classes resume, some teachers try to call parents at night, beginning several weeks before school starts. Typically, the teacher might say something like, "I just wanted to introduce myself. I'm delighted to have your son or daughter in my class this year. These are some of the things we'll be working on. Is there anything special I need to know: allergies, foods to avoid, concerns or circumstances I should be aware of? I'm looking forward to seeing you at the Open House on September 20." One teacher mails a little welcoming card to students' homes, telling them how much she is looking forward to meeting them on the first day of school.

Several schools have a Getting to Know Your New Teacher Day before the school year begins. These are usually informal so that the students and parents can meet the teacher and see their classroom. One advantage of holding this event before school officially begins is that the meeting cannot turn into an impromptu conference of "How's my child doing?" because the teacher doesn't yet know the student. Another advantage is that parents are more likely to come to the formal Open House or respond to future contacts if they can already attach a name and face to their child's teacher.

Other schools invite parents to an informal Meet The Teacher Night as close to the beginning of school as possible. The most effective format I have seen is an announcement at the end of the school year giving the date for the informal Meet The Teacher Night the first week of school after summer vacation. New registrants are given the same invitation as they arrive throughout the summer. Parents are notified that teachers will briefly go over the course of study and mention special routines during a specified 20-minute period. Before and after the organized 20 minutes, students introduce their parents to the teacher and show them the classroom and school.

One teacher uses the 20 minutes to explain the kinds of things she will do during the year and what parents should look for on certain days (e.g., the weekly calendar). She explains that she has an open door policy, which means that parents are welcome to come into the classroom to watch or participate any time. Her message is clear: She tells parents she will be in regular contact with them, and she asks parents to call her at home or school or to send her a note if they can't come in person because she needs two-way communication to best help their children. She also asks parents to fill out the following questionnaire and send it back with their child. (The questionnaire is on a regular sheet of paper with plenty of space for answers.)

Dear Parent,

As we begin the school year, I invite you to help me help your child realize the personal and academic goals you would like him or her to reach. Please respond to the questions in as much detail as you can.

1. I'd like to see my child improve in . . .
2. My child will need special attention/help in . . .
3. To help my child, I would like to learn more about . . .
4. I'd like to see a school project or activity centered on . . .

Thank you for your assistance!

The teacher refers to the information from the first three questions at subsequent parent-teacher conferences and works with parents to target students' strengths and improve their weaknesses. From the fourth question, she often finds out a great deal about parents' talents and interests. She uses this information to ask them to help with various activities throughout the year or to suggest community speakers interested in a specific area of study.

Home Visits

For the past several years, I have been interested in finding teachers who, like me, accidentally stumbled on the value of home visits. Home visits are a sensitive issue in some districts because of increasing violence and the potential danger to teachers' safety. Obviously, good judgment needs to be exercised and school policy examined. Fortunately, however, there are regions in the United States and elsewhere where home visits are still possible.

One of my colleagues started her career by living in the community where she taught. She began walking home with groups of students for personal exercise and to find out where her students lived. The children got the idea that they'd like to have their teacher come to their house and somehow the idea grew. Some of the parents started asking her for lunch and she eventually was invited to recitals, tea, and a christening. My experience was similar. I believe it was a parent volunteer, the mother of one of my students, who first invited me for lunch. I mailed my student and his mother a thank-you card and gave an appreciative, glowing report in class. To my astonishment, several other invitations were issued almost immediately.

Other teachers have initiated home visits for professional reasons. One teacher was team teaching with three grade level colleagues. Her team started conducting joint parent-teacher conferences and then decided to arrange home visits with parents who could not come to the conference. They split into two groups and began home visits. Having a partner not only allowed them to feel safer but also kept the conversation flowing smoothly. However, they were particularly careful to set the parent at ease so a two-against-one impression would be avoided.

One teacher is a member of a staff that organizes home visits with every parent in its school at the beginning of the academic year. The teachers are sent out in groups of twos and are responsible for a certain number of homes in a given area. Still another teacher has found home visits a necessity. She teaches in an inner-city school with a very transient population. Phones are often disconnected when bills are not paid, or parents are so afraid the school will pass the telephone number to bill collectors that they will not divulge their number. The teacher usually sends notes home first or, if the parent is illiterate, she teaches the child how to use a tape recorder and sends notes home on cassette. If that doesn't elicit a response, she makes a home visit.

In another inner-city school, an exemplary teacher was frustrated by a student teacher's attitude toward the children and her comment that "at least in suburbia, all the children have clean hands." The teacher talked to her student teacher and gave the following sage advice, which she now passes on to all of her student teachers:

> Part of me sympathizes with you, but part of me sympathizes with the class. These are the children we have in our school. You need compassion to see there's a child underneath. Don't use the child's environment as an excuse. Realize you are not a miracle worker, even though you can sometimes work with agencies, but do your best while you have them at school.

School must be a safe haven where children can count on their teacher to care about them and their future. Teachers who have taught in both affluent and poor neighborhoods recognize that what they know about a child's life outside of school is at best incomplete: "Even a teacher who thinks she knows a child well doesn't *really* know that child. You don't know what's going on at home. Sometimes you can get a glimmer and you wonder how they survive."

Involving Parents

Meeting parents at the beginning of the school year is only the tip of the iceberg for teachers who believe that talking and working with parents is directly linked to children's success at school. Good teachers want parents to keep coming to school, even if it's just for a few minutes as they drop off their child or bring their child's project to school. These teachers watch for such opportunities and take advantage of them. As one explained, "I can get back to a lesson and I can get back to other things I am doing, but that parent might be gone. So if at all possible, I drop whatever I'm doing and talk to that parent."

A first- and second-grade teacher manages to get her students to think that having their parents come to school is a wonderful reward. She says,

> Now, if I meet with your parents, that means I know you're doing a really good job. I'll be able to show them all these wonderful things you're doing and we'll be able to work together to make it better for you. The kids usually go home and tell their parents, "My teacher said you need to go to school." I usually end up meeting with most parents and I think a lot of that is because I make the effort to let them know, "I want you here!"

Sometimes, parents can be involved at home. Normally, homework is discouraged in first grade, but one first-grade teacher has spent her own money to buy all kinds of small books she lets the children take home when they can "read" the book (sometimes by memory). The children think that getting one of the teacher's books is a great privilege. The teacher knows parents are listening to the children because her students come back and say, "My Mommy liked that story I read last night." Occasionally, parents ask for additional homework for their six-year-old. Instead of replying that the school or district frowns on homework for first-grade students, this teacher sends home little sets of math flashcards. Flashcards are also frowned on in her district, but she values parents' willingness to help, their interest in the child, and the implicit message to the child that school matters.

One of the best teachers I have ever seen was very creative in figuring out ways to involve parents. One time, she used recipes as a catalyst. When the children were studying fractions in math class, the teacher sent home a note asking parents to have the child copy their favorite food recipe. She then created an *Our Class's Favorite Recipes* booklet for each child to decorate and take home. Both the children and their parents enjoyed reading the recipes and trying the various dishes, which represented an interesting international sample.

Another teacher found that having Students of the Week invite their family to school was a positive reason for parents to want to come to school. Doing so also uncovered some interesting family talents and helped her and the class know each other in a different way:

> A couple of years ago, I decided that on Friday afternoon, we'd invite the Student of the Week's family to come to the classroom. This was one of the most successful things I've ever implemented in my class. If they couldn't arrange to come in at that particular time, we rescheduled. Those children looked forward so much to their special time. They would write out a little invitation and send it home, and parents would come in and share wonderful things. Moms and Dads came in, brothers and sisters if they could, and they shared a favorite story or a poem. Sometimes they just talked to the kids. The other kids would often say, "Remember when So-and-So's Mom and Dad came in and they did whatever." It was a wonderful chance for students to share their home with the classroom.

A kindergarten teacher asks parents and community professionals to help her with an annual theme that culminates in an evening musical for the community. One theme, for example, was birds. The teacher and her team partner had parents helping children at 10 activity centers. One of the parents taught the class sign language for the song, "Six Little Ducks"; another had the students use shaving cream to print the colors of birds; one parent with a Ph.D. in mathematics taught measurement using gummy worms and bird lengths; and still another parent who runs a business to take care of sick birds brought some healthy birds to school to use as teaching models. While the children were working, the teachers videotaped them so that after the evening musical, parents who were not able to be in the classroom could see their children on videotape.

A fourth-grade teacher responsible for teaching state history decided to involve parents in a unique way. She created a Discover Our State list of free or inexpensive tours, trips, and attractions within the state and invited parents to take their children to them instead of to the usual amusement parks. When the children came back to school, they reported what they had learned:

> Last year, I told the kids they could use video camcorders [if they had them]. I had two or three who were very creative: "Hello, my name is Ben and here I am reporting from beautiful Fern Lake. Now this is an example of . . ."—very much like you would see on a newsreel. They were just hysterical. Even the parents thanked me, because there are so many places right around here that are quite a learning experience. The parents, then, are a part of the child's work and they learn a lot going along.

Schools routinely ask parents to sign up at Open House if they are willing to accompany students on field trips, help with sports days, assist in the library, and the like. But teachers have raised several issues specifically concerning parent volunteers for classroom teachers. One teacher, who was a parent volunteer while raising her own children, is now very careful to ask her volunteers what kind of work they prefer and whether they prefer to help in the classroom or work at home. She believes that, like her students, adults have specific strengths and that people are happiest doing what they enjoy.

Several teachers commented that they love to have adults in the room with them because word quickly spreads in communities and parent volunteers can be powerful advocates for teachers. (Of course, the opposite can also be true.) The teachers also mentioned that having parents in the room is a wonderful barometer for monitoring what they say to students, how they treat students, and how their teaching and behavior affects students. In addition to team teaching in open spaces, it was from having parent volunteers in the classroom that teachers became accustomed to—in fact, came to enjoy—having the public watching and appreciating what they are doing for students.

A number of schools have a Curriculum Night during the fall semester. This is quite different from Open House and is an attempt to help parents understand their child's curriculum and how it is delivered. Although children are not usually invited, I have seen children selected to demonstrate how specific activity centers work or to teach parents a skill such as editing a writing sample on their computer. One kindergarten teacher "teaches" parents at the Curriculum Night how to focus on the purpose of reading: whether it's for word recognition, understanding the concept of print, enjoyment, getting clues from illustrations, or so forth. In one school, these Curriculum Nights were offered on a monthly basis to keep parents informed.

Recently, another school tried a Parents in School Night in early November. The evening included a choice of 45-minute workshops suggested or requested by parents. The workshops included choices such as "Espanol es fabuloso!—Learn about this exciting foreign language program"; "Fourth Grade Proficiency Testing—Learn everything you wanted to know about the test your 4th grader will be taking this year"; "Discipline Without Tears—Parents will learn some discipline techniques that won't cause you or your child tears"; "Gangs—What are gangs? What can you do to prevent your child from being involved in a gang?" There were door prizes, refreshments provided by the Parent Teacher Association, and free child care. Each parent received a letter of invitation and an RSVP sheet indicating their workshop selections. The letter ended with, "Show your child learning is a lifetime job. Be there!"

This same school also came up with a creative way to involve parents and take back their playground, an open field behind the school:

> Our playground was getting to be a drug haven and after school hours, the kids were really afraid to play there. So we got a group together to play football. We've got parents walking through the place all the time now.

Parent-Teacher Conferences

Preparation for parent-teacher conferences can occur long before the actual meeting takes place. As I mentioned earlier, the teacher who hands out the little questionnaire at the beginning of the year uses it later at the conference to discuss what the parent wants her to target in class. Together, she and the parent determine future goals for the child. Another teacher makes notes throughout the semester about specific areas to teach individual parents at the parent-teacher conference:

> This morning I had a little girl who's ready to read. She knows her letters, can follow lines, has the concept of print, [but] has no understanding of an initial sound. So I made a note that when the Mom comes in for the conference, I need to explain to her how to help the little girl be aware of beginning sounds through incidental teaching opportunities. Here is this parent who knew enough to teach her child the alphabet and how to write her name but now doesn't seem to know what comes next.

Most exemplary teachers do not wait until the official parent-teacher conferences that are normally scheduled immediately before or after release of the fall semester report card. They simply schedule conferences on an as-needed basis, particularly if the student is having difficulty in some area.

I have yet to hear any exemplary teacher claim to be good at parent-teacher conferences. " 'Teachers are trained extensively in how to communicate with children. They receive little or no training and in-service development in how to communicate openly, honestly, and accessibly with parents' " (Alexander, cited in Hargreaves, 1995, p. 19). Several colleagues and I have had the opportunity to learn from some very skilled teachers or counselors because we participated in the conferences as team partners with them. As one colleague said, "You learn a *lot* by watching. The more you get to see somebody else do it, the more you see what needs to be done."

Another teacher commented that one of the best lessons she learned was to focus on one or two things parents can do rather than bewildering them by rambling through a whole range of possibilities. Other teachers commented on how important it is to make parents feel comfortable by not talking down to them or using education jargon. These teachers have learned to give parents precise comments and specific, concrete suggestions for what they can do to help the child. As one teacher noted, "Most parents want to help. They just sometimes don't know what to do or don't have the means or don't want to interfere. And that's why it's so important for them not to be intimidated by the school but to be welcomed. They need to feel that they can come in and ask any question. Whether it seems silly or not, it needs to be asked."

For several years I had the opportunity to observe a teacher who was very skilled at keeping the focus of the conference on how to help the child. She was able to get the parent to talk about the child and she was a superb listener. For example, she found that asking parents what the child is talking about at home revealed what the child was interested in and sometimes indicated what the child had internalized at school and could explain at home. When she also found out what particularly interested the child, she used the information to suggest writing topics or projects for that child.

Feeling empathy for parents, making them comfortable, listening to parents, and keeping parental assistance clear and concise are invaluable tips. Teachers are tempted to make general statements like, "Katie's having trouble reading," rather than finding a specific area in which the parent really can help make a difference. Part of communicating well with parents is knowing them well enough to know what you can say, although honesty is important: "If kids are having a hard time, you have to be honest with the parents because whitewashing doesn't do anybody any good. If you do not let them know, you're doing a disservice to the kid and maybe to the parents." That does not mean that the truth has to be all negative; it does mean that careful and specific examples, evidence, or suggestions are needed to support teachers' claims:

> We had a parent say, "I don't really enjoy coming and hearing nothing but bad junk about my kids." She has seven boys. Father is not anywhere nearby and she's been in jail for drugs and is just now allowed to have custody of the children. They've been with a great-grandmother, a grandmother, an uncle, back to a grand-mother, back to great-grandmother . . . She [the mother] almost broke down because the boys are in trouble all the time. She said, "I know people here maybe don't think I care, but I do get upset when I have to come in and hear nothing but bad things about the boys." I told her Shalil is not misbehaving in my room and I'm very glad that he isn't. When he misbehaves, it's on the bus or the playground because his brothers have talked him into it. Not that I'm going to lie. I'm going to say, "He's hitting and beating up kids, but what I would like you to deal with is . . ." I'm going to find something that the child *can* do better and that Mother can do to help the child.

Teachers can sometimes feel as hurt and defensive as this parent. One teacher had a parent enter her room, leap to an unwarranted conclusion, and attempt to intimidate her. In another school, a parent arrived for his conference, but before sitting down, he leaned close to the young teacher and said, "If you give me any problems, I'm going to be in your face."

However, most parents want the best for their children. It is not unusual for them to ask parenting questions unrelated to academic issues. One parent came to a meeting in tears with a discipline question. A seasoned teacher who has worked for years to improve her parent-teacher conferences said,

> I learned very young that if I didn't have an answer, I can be compassionate and I can be understanding. Many times, that's what parents need the most. I might say, "I will keep in mind that your child is struggling with this during the day." Just that kind of connection can help. You've got to learn to deal with people. It's not always just the reading, writing, and arithmetic. You need to learn how to read people and judge people, how to say things diplomatically, how to be tactful and still be to the point.

As we will see in the next chapter, using interpersonal knowledge to structure the social environment of classrooms and involve parents often overlaps with the use of teachers' intrapersonal knowledge. Teachers' intrapersonal knowledge has to do with understanding themselves and others and includes dispositions and ethics that exemplary teachers believe are vitally important to learning within and beyond the classroom.

Intrapersonal Knowledge

5

Structuring the Environment for the Development of Ethics and Dispositions

Each is inspired to develop himself more completely as he sees admirable qualities, not fully realized in himself, manifest in another whom he esteems.

Nancy Sherman (1989, p. 142)

Mary Beaupre leaned on her shopping cart, trying to decide which card to buy for Mr. Schmidt, the senior citizen reading volunteer who had so faithfully come to her classroom every week.

"Hi, Ms. Beaupre! Do you still remember me?"

Mary turned to look at the grinning teenager beside her. "Why, of course," she said with pleasure. "Kevin Ng! I can't believe how tall you are! Are you still pitching for the summer team?"

"Yeah, I'm doing a good job, but our team's not likely going to the playoffs this year. We lost some of our best hitters when school let out, you know."

After a few minutes of conversation, Kevin's voice hesitated as he said, "Ms. Beaupre, do you remember Val from our class?"

Dear, wonderful Val Ivanko! How could anyone forget the fun-loving student from Russia. Mary remembered how quickly he had mastered

English and how she was the only one he allowed to call him Vladimir because she had practiced dozens of times with him until she had mastered the accent and rolled the "r" to his satisfaction. "Didn't he move to the Carolinas after sixth grade?" she asked Kevin. Kevin nodded and kept his head lowered.

"I was mowing Mr. Fenwick's grass yesterday. Val's family lived between him and me, you know."

Mary knew how close Kevin and Val had become, both as brilliant academic competitors in class and fiercely loyal teammates on the ball field. She felt icy fingers of fear as she watched Kevin's facial muscles tighten. There was a long pause.

"Apparently Mr. Ivanko called Mr. Fenwick last week to ask him for Dr. Van Erkel's number. Val has bone cancer and is in the hospital. It sounds really bad."

Mary drove home in a daze and went to the carved sideboard where she kept pictures of all of her classes, along with notes and mementos from former students. Her hands stroked the cool surface of the wooden nesting dolls Val had proudly given her and as she stared at Val's teasing blue eyes and unruly blond hair in his sixth-grade photo, she kept wondering why. Why a child? Why Val? Her heart heavy, she began to prepare dinner.

The next few days were a blur as Mary called Mr. Fenwick and the doctor to find out the Ivanko's city and their telephone number. Night after night, she called their number but there was never anyone home. She sighed as she hung up the phone yet again.

"Why don't you call the operator and get the hospital number?" suggested her husband, Paul.

Three hospitals later, Mary had still not found Val. In desperation, she said to the hospital receptionist, "If your son had bone cancer, what hospital would he likely be in?"

"Our Lady of Grace," was the prompt reply. "I can give you that number if you like, but it's always busy."

Sure enough, several days went by before Mary finally reached the hospital switchboard operator. Her heart leaped when she found out Val was there and her hand gripped the receiver as the call rang through to his room.

"Hello," said a woman's weary voice that Mary recognized immediately.

"Oh! Mrs. Ivanko, this is Mary Beaupre. I taught Val in sixth grade. Kevin Ng told me Val is sick."

"I no speak good English," Mrs. Ivanko replied. "You write Val letter maybe?"

"Oh, thank you!" Mary began. She was relieved when a nurse picked up the phone to give her the hospital address.

Mary sat at the table, pen poised, but unable to write. Frustrated, she picked up her guitar and began humming the Russian ballad Val had sung for the class one day. In her mind, she heard his clear soprano voice soaring across the haunting melody and understood the homesickness he was feeling. Val had always loved music class and had confided to her later that the songs had helped him learn English. As the ballad came to an end, Paul put down his newspaper and leaned back against the sofa. He loved listening to Mary practice for school or community performances. He was surprised this time to hear her start, but not finish, a sequence of six or eight pieces.

"What's wrong, sweetheart? Letter not working out?"

"I can't write what I want to say," she answered with a faraway look. "Nothing's happening, so I thought maybe I could sing a tape for Val. He always loved music. Problem is, I don't know what kind of music he'd like now. Kids that age change so fast."

"Mary, I know you're trying to please Val, but you can't second-guess his tastes. And it really doesn't matter what you pick. All he needs to hear is that you love him and that you're there beside him helping him be strong. He'll hear it in your voice no matter what you sing for him."

Mary gave Paul a grateful glance and turned on the tape recorder. Her beautiful voice rose and fell as she sang tunes she had taught Val's class, hummed his poignant Russian ballad, and added some new songs she had learned for the school's recent fund-raising event. As the shadows deepened, her voice strengthened over the words, "You are my hero" and hovered gently over the final phrase, "You are the wind beneath my wings." Tears streamed down her face as she leaned forward to remove the cassette tape.

Seven weeks later, a box arrived at the Beaupre house. On top of the newspaper packing lay a letter with unfamiliar handwriting.

Dear Ms. Beaupre,

I was Val's nurse and I'm writing this letter on behalf of Mr. and Mrs. Ivanko. They want you to know how much your tape meant to Val. He was forever telling us wonderful stories about you and I almost feel like I know you. Val truly was the most courageous child I have ever nursed and at the end, when the morphine wasn't working anymore, he'd ask me to put on your tape so he could rest. He always smiled when he got to the humming song and before he got too weak, he'd sing it with you. Enclosed is Val's favorite teddy bear for you. It's his parents' way of saying thank you.

Yours truly,

Brenda Craven, RN

P. S. I wish my kids could have you for their teacher.

Exemplary Teaching and Intrapersonal Knowledge

This chapter briefly examines some facets of intrapersonal knowledge that are particularly pertinent to teaching: reflection and the development of ethics and dispositions. Although we freely use the terms *reflection, ethics,* and *dispositions* as educators and although they appear to be closely intertwined, they can have many different meanings for teachers and parents. Reflection is discussed in a separate section, but it will become obvious that reflection is related to ethics and dispositions.

For the purpose of this book, I am defining a disposition as "an attributed characteristic of a teacher, one that summarizes the trend of a teacher's actions in particular contexts. . . . The acts that constitute a disposition may be conscious and deliberate or so habitual and 'automatic' that they seem intuitive or spontaneous" (Katz & Raths, 1985, p. 301). If, for example, we describe someone as "curious," we have seen this disposition on enough occasions to expect curiosity to be evident in this person on a regular basis.

When I use the term *ethics,* I am referring to universal ideals that philosophers have come to recognize as necessary for a peaceful, just, and civil society. In short, certain ethics contribute to making individuals and the world a better place. The ethics mentioned in this book are not exhaustive. They include only those specifically mentioned by this particular sample of teachers. I have tried throughout the book to illustrate how these ethics can be modeled, so the following treatment offers simply brief explanations or new examples to refresh the reader's memory.

Sometimes the terms *morals* and *values* are used interchangeably with ethics. For example, the development of ethics is generally referred to in philosophy and psychology as moral development. These terms can have negative and sometimes explosive overtones, particularly in the United States. I refer to morals as behaviors or qualities valued by a certain community of people, but not necessarily accepted at a more universal level. On the other hand, universal ethics may be extolled as good morals by smaller communities. They have also been called *virtues* or *character* (Sherman, 1989). Aristotle thought that character had to do with "a person's enduring traits; that is, with the attitudes, sensibilities, and beliefs that affect how a person sees, acts, and indeed lives" (Sherman, 1989, p. 1). If teaching, no matter where it occurs, reflects teachers' attitudes, sensibilities, and beliefs, then we can argue that the development of ethics and dispositions plays an important role in teaching and education (also see Goodlad, Soder, & Sirotnik, 1990; Jackson, Boostrom, & Hansen, 1993; Sergiovanni, 1992).

What form that role ought to take, and how we agree or disagree with it in relation to our children and our nation, has been, and continues to be, the basis of many heated debates. Starratt (1991) summarized the growing interest and concern of academicians in his article "Building an Ethical School" and comments that "the literature may be yet a step away from speaking concretely enough to practitioners" (p. 186). Practitioners, however, do not wait for the literature and in the meantime do not teach in a vacuum. The exemplary teachers in this book, aware of the academic and public debates, have independently come to their own conclusions and are trying to develop specific dispositions and ethics in their students. In other words, they are structuring the classroom so that they can teach their intrapersonal knowledge in a way they consider appropriate for children.

This is not a case of "do as I say, not as I do," even though the teachers do not necessarily achieve their own ideal vision of ethical development. This is a case of asking their students only to do what they, as teachers, continue to work toward in their own development. Although each disposition or ethic they mentioned is worthy of much deeper treatment, I have selected only short descriptions that attempt to capture the teachers' meaning and portray facets of each disposition or ethic that may be less common than those described in teachers college texts.

When I asked two random samples of teachers to describe what an exemplary teacher means to them, their descriptions included the following: *innovative, curious, constantly learning, optimistic, dedicated, creative, flexible, caring, good communicators* (Collinson, 1991, 1994). Their perceptions closely parallel characteristics of exemplary teachers described in the literature (e.g., Easterly, 1983; Mertz, 1987; Penick, Yager, & Bonnstetter, 1986; Shanoski & Hranitz, 1989; Stone, 1987; Van Schaack & Glick, 1982). If these descriptors, along with other dispositions and ethics described later in this chapter, portray the legacy of exemplary teachers to their students, then teachers' intrapersonal knowledge ought to be getting more attention than it currently does in research and in teacher education programs. However, our discussions of teaching are "nearly devoid of talk about . . . the profound importance of teachers to the moral development of students. It is as if the moral dimensions of teaching were lost, forgotten . . . or simply taken for granted" (Fenstermacher, 1990, p. 132). This chapter focuses on those aspects of intrapersonal knowledge that exemplary teachers deem so important that they not only attempt to improve them in their own development but also try to model them for their students.

I am not suggesting that these teachers are paragons of virtue. They would be the first to say that, although they try hard to do their best, there are days when their best doesn't measure up to their expectations and that they've had some failures they would rather forget. They would also say there is a great deal of room for improvement every day and that there are always other possibilities to pursue. What I am saying, however, is that the performance of experienced, exemplary teachers, "though not necessarily perfect," can nevertheless provide us with "exemplary performances from which we can learn" (Berliner, 1986, p. 6).

We can also learn by examining exemplary teachers' perceptions of what helped them improve their teaching. Studying excellent teachers is logical if we are seriously interested in an ideal of excellence for our nation's teachers and in ethical ideals for our students so that "each is inspired to develop himself more completely as he sees admirable qualities, not fully realized in himself, manifest in another whom he esteems" (Sherman, 1989, p. 142).

Reflection as Intrapersonal Knowledge

Reflection became part of our educational jargon in the 1980s, and although it was recognized and promoted as something desirable for both teachers and students, it means many things to teachers. Drawing on Dewey's (1933/1960) work, I define reflection here as the familiar six-step process of inquiry:

1. Recognition of a problem
2. Proposal of one or more hypotheses
3. Inquiry (gathering of pertinent information)
4. Reasoning (e.g., analysis of information and predicting potential consequences of actions or inaction)
5. Decision making to resolve the problem
6. Evaluation of whether and how the process could have been improved

Dewey (1933/1960) recognized, however, that judgment also plays an important role in reflection, for implicit in reflection is increasing wisdom to recognize which facts are pertinent, wisdom to reason one's way through the situation, and wisdom to know when to act or not to act. This same idea is captured in the prayer attributed to St. Francis of Assisi: "God, grant me the serenity to accept the things I cannot change, courage to change the things I can, and wisdom to know the difference."

Dewey (1933/1960) also noted that our judgment depends on our prior experiences. His idea was summarized in Miriani's (McShane, 1995) discussion of critical analysis of art: "With knowledge, you have more understanding and with more understanding, you can make a better judgment" (p. 15A). This thinking parallels teachers' reasons for getting to know children: Knowing them as individuals fosters understanding and understanding allows careful judgment of how best to help each child learn.

We should not be deceived into thinking that reflection is an exclusively intellectual process devoid of emotion. In the next chapter, we will see how exemplary teachers structure the intellectual environment on a foundation of reflection, but we will also see how important the cultivation of dispositions and ethics are to this process:

> Buchman argues that contemplation is a central factor in developing teachers' abilities to practice their profession in a considerate, service-oriented manner. Indeed, she emphasizes that thinking and moral virtue are intertwined and that, together, they enable persons to engage in acts of caring service. This, in her view, is essential to excellent teaching. (Beck, 1994, p. 56)

Part of reasoning, for example, involves learning about learning, an intensely personal process. Jackson (1987) emphasized the important connections between reflection and dispositions as two key components of learning to learn:

> In cognitive terms, this means teaching a person to reason, to make judgments, to develop sustained arguments, to criticize the arguments of others, and so forth. . . . In terms more dispositional than cognitive, it means equipping the would-be learner with those attitudinal and emotional attributes . . . that predispose a person to the use of reason. These include a keen sense of curiosity, a high degree of intellectual honesty, self-confidence in one's ability to acquire knowledge, a healthy degree of skepticism when confronted with the knowledge claims of others, and so forth. . . . Taken together, these two components of learning to learn, the cognitive and the dispositional, add up to a readily recognizable intellectual posture. (p. 49)

These and other dispositions are vital to good thinking (see Ennis, 1987 for a taxonomy of critical thinking dispositions).

Socrates claimed that "the unexamined life is not worth living." Through reflection, the teachers in this book have examined their teaching and their own development to find out what gives meaning to their lives as teachers. They understand why they make certain instructional decisions and they can give reasons for their decisions. They have also described the following ethics and dispositions as important to the quality of their own lives and, they believe, to their students' lives within and beyond the classroom.

An Ethic of Care

Compassion and Empathy

Van Schaack and Glick (1982) were among the first to note that exemplary teachers demonstrate a genuine ethic of caring about children.

> Such an ethic focuses on the demand of relationships. . . . One becomes whole when one is in relationship with another and with many others. . . . [An ethic of care] requires fidelity to persons, a willingness to acknowledge their right to be who they are, an

openness to encountering them in their authentic individuality, a loyalty to the relationship, . . . a level of caring that honors the dignity of each person and desires to see that person enjoy a fully human life. (Starratt, 1991, p. 195)

Part of an ethic of care also includes compassion for others. Compassion is

the glue that binds together everything that we do in education. . . . You need only examine your own significant learning experiences to validate the crucial importance that compassion plays in education. . . . How else can children learn to care about themselves if they do not feel such compassion and love from you, their teacher? (Zehm & Kottler, 1993, pp. 9-10)

Although many circumstances evoke compassion in the school context, perhaps the one most frequently dealt with by teachers is death. Teacher preparation programs do not generally prepare teachers to deal with death, but death is a part of every teacher's career, whether it's the loss of a student from a childhood disease, a car accident, or a drive-by shooting; the death of a student's grandparent; the death of a colleague's parent or spouse; the loss of a child's beloved pet—the list goes on and on. Children think very deeply about death and an afterlife, and although some of their understanding is misconceived, most of them grasp that such momentous loss calls for compassion.

Children do not necessarily know how to show compassion and need to have it modeled. For example, when a kindergarten teacher returned to class after the death of her mother, she was startled when, throughout the morning, her students blurted out comments such as "I had a fish once that died" or "My cat died when I was three." It took her awhile to realize that these children were trying to extend sympathy and practice empathy. She stopped the regular activities and invited the children to express their thoughts, recognizing that although her students were dutifully going through the motions of learning, they were preoccupied with her loss and wanted to make contact at the most fundamental human level.

Young children do not yet have the vocabulary to convey their deep feelings and fears about death, but as the vignette in Chapter 4 illustrates, art can play a powerful role in letting children communicate their concerns to adults. Above all, whenever a death occurs, children in the class need to be assured that they will be taken care of and that if they want to, they may talk about death and the person who died.

Respect for Self and Others

> In order for children to open up and trust you, they must feel that you accept them as people. . . . Acceptance of others requires a great degree of tolerance, sensitivity, and cultural awareness. It means that you are knowledgeable about diverse backgrounds from which your children originate, and you demonstrate respect for their individual and cultural differences. When you can model this in your own behavior, then you can teach children to be tolerant of one another's differences. (Zehm & Kottler, 1993, p. 48)

Finding and articulating students' strengths is one form of respect because it indicates that the teacher knows the students as unique individuals.

For the same reason, teachers want their students to see them as human beings too and they do not hesitate to tell their class about their pets or that they are going to graduate school or that they love football. When one teacher heard her students calling each other derogatory names, she told them how such a name had hurt her deeply as a child. These teachers seem to intuit that knowing a person is somehow linked to caring about and respecting that person.

Trust is also a form of respect, and exemplary teachers are not afraid to let students know that respect and trust are what they expect in the classroom. They do not abuse their position of authority toward this end, knowing full well that both respect and trust are earned. Although they do verbalize their expectations when the opportunity arises (as in the name-calling incident), they count on their hard work, honesty, fairness, care, and integrity to earn the respect of their students and colleagues:

> Trust plays a big role in my room. The students trust me and I trust them. When that trust is broken, we work through it. Why was it broken? What can we do to trust each other again? I had a child stealing recently and it really broke that trusting feeling in the room. We worked through that and now he's not doing it anymore. That's not to say that he might not try it again, but it probably will be a long time before he tries it again, at least in my room. I seriously doubt he'd want to break that trust again because he saw

how my lack of confidence in him hurt the class. We work as a team to make the room a positive environment.

Teachers are not immune to feeling hurt by the lack of respect and trust in them that they perceive in the media and the public. They seize opportunities to help their public know and understand what they are doing:

> A neighbor down the road told me that he wouldn't support a school levy. When I said, "Well you better, because it affects you," he said, "No it doesn't!" "Absolutely," I said. "These kids are the leaders that are going to be in charge of our country when you get old. You'd better hope that the brightest and the best are out there working for *you.*" His way of apology was that he bought me a set of stamps for the class. But it seems like the public really doesn't understand what you deal with. They don't understand that sometimes just a nice letter from a parent can lift your spirits so you'll do 100% more than you ever thought you could because you've got this "somebody out there appreciates me" kind of feeling.

Understanding Self and Others

> Arthur Jesild (1955) was among the first of modern-day educators to focus attention on the connection between the teacher's personal life and her or his professional effectiveness. Jesild maintained that understanding yourself is the single most important task in the growth toward developing healthy attitudes of self-acceptance. The influence of his little book was short-lived. Shortly after it was published, Sputnik, the first space flight, was launched by the Russians. The nation began a frenzied focus, not on teachers' needs but on the perceived national security imperative to train teachers of scientists and technicians. The human dimensions of teaching or learning were considered too soft to be of great priority. (Zehm & Kottler, 1993, p. 3)

Particularly within the last decade, however, there has been a closer examination of how teachers think, reason, and affect learning (or lack of learning) in students. Human dimensions of teaching are again under scrutiny, with authors linking self-understanding and excellent teaching (e.g., Berman, 1987; Heath, 1986; Waller, 1965; Westerhoff, 1987; Willie & Howey, 1980).

Gardner (1963/1981) described self-knowledge as systematically seeking to develop "the full range of [one's] capacities for sensing, wondering, learning, understanding, loving and aspiring" (pp. 11-12). This development contributes to teachers' ability to sort out what gives meaning to life. Bolin (1987) also pointed out that self-understanding is necessary to support teachers' commitment to the profession: "To sustain one's vision, one must attend to one's own being and nurture those personal factors that prompted vocational choice" (p. 219). On a practical note, self-understanding has been associated with flexibility in the classroom: "The better people understand themselves, the less likely they are to be overwhelmed by events they cannot control" (Redl & Wattenberg, 1959, p. 494). Also, until teachers can effectively use reflection to understand what they do and why they do it, their ability to understand students and colleagues may be curtailed.

Giving to and Receiving From Others

Describing teachers' collaboration to improve teaching, Lieberman and Miller (1990) observed that "it is the personal interaction rather than the instructional interaction that is most valued" (p. 159). Throughout this book, there have been numerous examples indicating that this observation is also valid for students.

We might expect that teachers, by the nature of their job, would give a great deal to their students. But exemplary teachers seem to go well beyond the call of duty. One wrote a grant to fund the purchase of big books for her class. Another worked with a committee to phone or write companies that could give "freebies" to teachers at an upcoming literacy conference. These teachers routinely spend evenings or Saturdays at the local public library or at bookstores to find books for children. They may also spend their personal money on items for the classroom:

> I saw most of my kids reading these neat sci-fi books like *My Teacher Fried My Brains*. One of my boys, who was basically not a reader, was coming up to me every night with "Do you know what happens next in this chapter?" We didn't have too many sci-fi books, so I went to the bookstore and selected three or four. I bought them and gave them to the [school] library under the stipulation that my class could take them out as many times as

they wanted before the rest of the students could have them. My kids enjoyed that.

Teachers have for many years reached out to the community to ask for help. One teacher commented that "there are lots of community things available. You just have to dig." She has invited guest speakers, firefighters, a senior citizen dance group, and clowns:

> We had a group of clowns from a Moose lodge one time. We had a sleep-over at school as a second- and third-grade reward on a Friday night. We spent all night in the gym with the kids and we had these clowns come and entertain. They came free of charge; we just had to give a donation to the lodge.

The teachers recognize that they need to receive from others to learn and teach well. They regularly ask colleagues or parents for information and assistance: "How do you think this will work?" or "How would you go about doing this?" They appreciate the give and take, particularly with like-minded colleagues:

> I really like sharing with colleagues back and forth about what's going on with the kids, sharing knowledge, sharing materials or saying, "I've got this new book. Have you seen it?" I even like when they want to make sure that I'm feeling good or say "Hey, that's a good job!"

But what teachers really like receiving is a note or a visit from former students. They appreciate having had the opportunity to contribute to the growth and development of a child:

> It's always fun when the kids who have moved on come back to see you. It's refreshing to look at them from a distance when you don't see them on a day-to-day basis. Those are the rewards—to see the children and see how they've matured and how they've grown. It's really fascinating.

One teacher keeps little notes from students in her purse to read on days when things are not going well. These teachers recognize they are the sum of all the lives who have touched them, and they want in some small way to affect the lives of their young students. Their thinking is perhaps best reflected in the verse attributed to Flavia: "Some people come into our lives and quickly go. Some stay for awhile and leave footprints on our hearts and we are never the same."

Courage

Van Schaack and Glick (1982) describe exemplary teachers as "strong individuals; they have deep convictions and courage; they take risks" (p. 36). Gardner (1963/1981) also linked courage to risk taking. Sometimes courage involves being vulnerable on a personal level. For example, one teacher withdrew her participation in a community tradition, an annual talent show to raise money for the school, when she realized that the jokesters represented blatant racism. Disappointing people in the community and giving them the impression that she didn't care about the school hurt her, but her convictions were very strong. She explained her reasoning publicly, and when she was not supported, she realized that her integrity mattered more to her than popular opinion.

Most often for teachers, courage involves professional risk. One teacher refused to implement a particular strategy the principal wanted. She explained why she could not teach what she had reason to believe would harm or hinder children's learning. At the same time, she knew that her principal was likely to give her a poor recommendation when she transferred to another school.

Another teacher proposed having parent-teacher conferences in the late afternoon and evening so that more parents could come to school. Her principal and the staff supported her idea and kept data on the results. There was about a 50% rise in participation. When the central administration found out what the school was doing, they stopped the practice, claiming it "gave the public the impression that the teachers were getting the day off." Knowing that "the administration always wins," the teacher nonetheless prepared an argument and presented it to the district's Reform Panel, if only to be on the record.

A Work Ethic

Work Ethic and Pride of Effort

I've mentioned several times how rewarding it is to teachers to see growth in children thanks to the teacher's and student's efforts. Several exemplary teachers associate hard work with an ethic of care, an idea shared by Noddings (1994): "Caring implies competence. When we genuinely care, we want to do our very best to effect worthwhile results for the recipients of our care" (p. ix).

Teachers model their personal work ethic when they make good use of their students' time and when they provide challenging material instead of "busy work." One teacher devises interesting little games to review Spanish numbers and colors for the foreign language teacher as her students are waiting in line at the washroom or drinking fountain after recess. Several teachers mentioned that they not only want to communicate a love of learning to their students, they want children to learn that hard work can be fun and rewarding:

> A lot of learning is very hard work. I want them to get used to [the idea] that it's fun, it's hard work, and when you're done, you feel great about it. . . . Fun is being involved and making your mind go 'round and producing something you're proud of. When [you're] finished, [you're] really *proud*. (Collinson, 1994, p. 83)

Dedication and Perseverance

When we watch an outstanding performance in athletics or the arts or in any other area, we can be fairly certain that we are seeing the culmination of years of perseverance to develop a particular skill or talent. This high level of skill generally indicates that the performers had an overriding goal and an inner motivation, both of which helped them get through difficult times and accept personal sacrifices or hard choices along the way. Part of their motivation may be that they or someone they deeply admire thinks that the goal is worth pursuing. Trying to reach the goal then gives meaning to their lives.

What keeps exemplary teachers in teaching is the belief that children can learn and that teachers can make a difference. "Sometimes you don't know that you've made a difference until they come back to visit you." Children's comments, notes from parents, and wondering what it would be like to be the parent of a child a teacher had given up on—these are some of the motivations that help teachers persevere. Similarly, teachers encourage their students to persevere with skills, interests, and dreams.

Doing One's Best

" 'In order for [teachers] to give their best they must be aware of their strengths and the confidence others have in them' " (Johnson, cited in Beck, 1994, p. 56). If this is true for teachers, it is equally so for students. Just as creativity thrives in a supportive, open-minded environment, so does the desire to do one's best. Earlier, I noted that exemplary teachers take pains to point out students' strengths and make them public. Competition usually allows only one individual or team to be the best. Recognition and support of each others' skills and strengths allows students to do their personal best *and* learn to help others do the same.

One teacher knew that she wanted to improve how she taught reading to her class. She was delighted to find out that a novice teacher who had recently been hired had a strong background in reading. Some teachers might have been tempted to dismiss his lack of classroom experience or worry that a novice might teach better than they did. But this teacher recognized that all of us can learn from knowledgeable people and that the new teacher could help her be a better reading teacher. Trying to do her best motivated her to seek help in areas she had judged as needing improvement and to continue learning from those who had strengths from which she could benefit. Such teachers also expect all children to try their best:

> I have high expectations for myself as well as for my students, but they're not so high that they're unrealistic. I mean, the class just *knows* that I'm not going to be pleased if they don't show me their best, and I know what their best is because I work with them individually and I observe them in a group. I accept what I feel is their best attempt at something.

Exemplary teachers often say, "How could we make that better?" I learned by accident from my students that the fastest way to get better projects was to let them see excellent samples by other students. We had spent considerable time on one particular project and the students had been free to consult or seek help from their peers at any time. Nevertheless, when the projects were finished, the students said, "Could you please put them on the back table so we can read each others' during spare time?" Only then did it occur to me that traditionally, when teachers hand back work, children who do not score high know that adults expect them to do better but simply don't know how to do so. I realized with chagrin that it surely would be impossible for these students to know what an outstanding paper or project looked like without having seen examples. A quick check of annual results indicated that my students' grades had not varied much from one year to the next. For them to do better, I had to show them what "better" looked like and then help them figure out what made the difference and how to improve their own work.

A Disposition Toward Continuous Learning

If there is an overarching disposition that is characteristic of exemplary teachers, it is a love of learning. They like being on the cutting edge, are usually the first to experiment with possibilities for improving their teaching, do not do things the same way twice, and are constantly on the alert to learn from others and find new ideas (Collinson, 1994). This does not mean that they don't repeat a wonderful idea. They do, but they usually figure out how to make it even better.

I am often amazed by how much personal time and money exemplary teachers spend on learning how to be better teachers. In many jobs, professional or technical training is paid by the employer and is considered part of the job requirements. Not so for much of what exemplary teachers select for professional renewal (Collinson, 1994). They do take advantage of what their districts offer, such as after-school workshops, the occasional substitute teacher replacement, or a small professional development stipend, but they go far beyond those opportunities by using their own money. One teacher arranged baby-sitting so she could attend a minicourse for 5 Saturdays. Another paid full conference registration but was able to attend only the weekend sessions because her district would not release her for sessions on weekdays.

These teachers tell their students when they are taking tennis lessons or a class at university because they want their students to know that learning does not stop with the receipt of a school diploma. For the same reason, they encourage parents to talk with their children about technical courses or job training that they take for business purposes. Learning is as much a part of exemplary teachers' careers as teaching. As one explained, "The minute I stop learning is the minute I'll die as a teacher." If teachers can instill a love of learning in their students, they realize that other tasks, such as helping children learn how to learn and how to interact appropriately with others, are much easier.

Curiosity and Creativity

Dewey (1916/1966, 1933/1960) believed that motivation or interests must be channeled into habits of discipline and thinking but that an attitude of curiosity or wonder is vital to the process. "Until we understand, we are, if we have curiosity, troubled, baffled, and hence moved to inquire" (Dewey, 1933/1960, p. 132). However, "unless transition to an intellectual plane is effected, curiosity degenerates or evaporates" (p. 39). Gardner (1963/1981) also recognized that children's wonderful gift of curiosity forms the foundation for lifelong learning. Like Dewey, he wanted students to cultivate "habits of mind that will be useful in new situations—curiosity, open-mindedness, objectivity, respect for evidence and the capacity to think critically" (p. 23). In addition to exemplary teachers' emphasis on reflection, it should come as no surprise that one of their favorite responses to children begins with "I wonder . . ." or "Why do you think that . . . ?"

Exemplary teachers' own curiosity about how to help students learn leads them to experiment with new materials or instructional practices. By doing so, they are trying to understand themselves and their students more deeply. "Creativity is at once both an intensely individual act of expression and a bridge that links us to the rest of the universe" (Weisburd, 1987, p. 298). I have already mentioned various creative ways that exemplary teachers attempt to involve parents in their children's education. Chapter 6 will provide examples of how these teachers promote curiosity and creativity in their classrooms. They seem to sense that children's (and adults') creative thinking can best blossom in an open-minded environment with the support of a person who encourages curiosity and creativity, cares about them, and has their best interests at heart (see also Fine, 1985).

Risk Taking

One of the most important things that exemplary teachers do is to structure a safe environment in which children are encouraged to take intellectual risks, make mistakes, and feel free to say, "I don't understand." These teachers model how to deal with their own and their students' mistakes openly and honestly.

When people are curious and innovative learners, risk taking is a habit; they try numerous ways to see what works. But taking this kind of risk requires separating "mistake" and "failure." Innovative learners do not see mistakes as failures or as something that lowers their worth as an individual but, rather, as something that didn't work and as an opportunity to learn. This same disposition is the one portrayed in the famous story about Edison. When a brash young reporter accused him of having failed in a thousand attempts to create a light bulb, Edison is said to have replied in surprise, "My dear young man, I have not failed. I have merely found a thousand ways that do not work." Similarly, students are encouraged to try a different approach or seek help from others if one of their attempts does not work.

Problem Finding and Solving

Problem finding and problem solving are two very different skills, both of which are important. Arlin (1975) operationally defined problem solving as the traditional Piagetian formal operations stage of cognitive development but suggests that problem finding may represent a fifth stage. She hypothesized that the problem solving stage is a necessary but not sufficient condition for the problem finding stage.

In the "traditional" classroom, fully formed problems (particularly in math) are usually given to children, and there is often one "right" answer. Problems in real life are rarely that simple; they are harder to articulate because of extraneous information and they may have many possible resolutions with varying consequences. For example, one teacher knew in general that she was having a noise problem in her room, but observation did not identify specifically why this particular class was noisy. She decided to tape record a couple of classes to find the source of the problem. Another teacher collected data from error patterns on tests to try to figure out where some of her students were making mistakes in their thinking.

The inquiry process to resolve problems can be effective and efficient only if the problem is clearly defined. In the example of parent-teacher conferences used in Chapter 4, the teachers learned to avoid general or vague comments like, "Tim's having trouble in math." What they really had learned to avoid was formulating ill-defined problems that defied specific suggestions to improve the student's learning.

When children come to teachers for help with a vague question or problem, exemplary teachers usually ask a series of questions to try to focus the problem. Sometimes the teachers' questions serve to clarify the difficulty enough for the student to continue. On other occasions, teachers will push for precision and reasoning. For example, in one classroom, the children one day had the choice of selecting work partners. A few minutes later, one unhappy group came running up to the teacher saying, "We're not getting along!" The teacher led them through the following questions: "Why aren't you getting along? What caused that? Did you make a good choice when you picked that partner? Are you going to pick that partner again? What will you do next time when you're working with somebody you don't like?"

When the problem is an academic one, the children are encouraged to try various sources, including their peers and helpful charts posted around the room, before asking the teacher. Some teachers refer to this as their "Ask three before me" policy. By doing this, teachers hope to teach children that there are multiple sources of help available and they are gently pushing the children toward independent learning rather than fostering dependence on the teacher.

Several teachers commented that they like to put the children into a lot of situations where they're working on problems of figuring out how to do what needs to be accomplished. They might have children research how court is conducted so they can re-create the trial of an historical character or they might have students rewrite a story to present as a play. The children then have to figure out how to construct a play, how to select lead actors, which sets and props they need, and which roles are required on and off stage. Earlier, I mentioned a fifth-grade class that was researching eclipses. The teacher knew the children were finding problems in the research by the quality of their questions. Occasionally, however, their questions were so poorly defined that readers on the Internet would say, "What do you mean by . . . ?" Students quickly learned that if they wanted help from others, their requests or questions had to be clear and precise.

Responsibility

Part of Dewey's conceptualization of reflection is the idea of *consequences*. After we gather information pertinent to the defined problem, there are often choices or alternative decisions we can make. Thinking through a decision involves careful prediction or consideration of potential consequences (good and bad, short-term and long-term) that could result from different courses of action. Once we make a decision, we are responsible for our actions. Even when knowledge is incomplete, it is not unusual to hear thoughtful teachers say, "Given the information I was able to find at that time, I made the best decision I could under the circumstances." Or you might hear them say, "There's no use crying over spilled milk. How can we make the best of it?"

Honesty and responsibility are hallmarks of maturity, and exemplary teachers work hard to help children learn to think about consequences before taking action. They also try to help children understand that telling the truth about a choice (such as stealing or hitting another child) is important for learning responsibility. Although excuses, avoidance, or blaming others are common reactions from children, teachers want students to learn that they have choices about how they behave and that certain choices have better outcomes or consequences than others.

Flexibility

Experienced teachers will agree with Redl and Wattenberg (1959) that "uncontrollable events are a fact of life in the classroom" (p. 494). Some teachers are annoyed; others rise to the challenge. As noted in Chapter 1, teachers at the highest levels of professional expertise and psychological development are flexible in various ways. They have learned to appreciate multiple perspectives and possibilities; they understand that knowledge may be contradictory and incomplete, but they can live with ambiguity; they have an integrative approach to thinking; and they encourage creativity, flexibility, and complex learning in their students (see Kramer, 1983; Leithwood, 1990; Reiman & Thies-Sprinthall, in press).

One young teacher learned that she does some of her best teaching when children bring or say something impromptu. Clearly, this requires astute listening, quick thinking, and creativity on the part of the teacher. Another highly experienced teacher also enjoys spur-of-the-moment learning opportunities:

> One kid, I remember, brought in a bird's egg. They knew that my bird was sitting on a nest, so they wanted to take their egg and put it into the nest. We talked about why birds kick eggs out of the nest and it was a very interesting discussion that we would not have gotten into had not that child brought the egg in. I didn't open my science book, but science came alive that day and it will stick

with them. I've always found that's how I get to know kids. They bring stuff in that interests them and it's just instant, honest learning.

Flexibility is sometimes linked to empathy or compassion in the literature (e.g., Hunt, 1971). In one class, for example, a teacher had two students whose parents had been murdered. A colleague, aware of the situation, was disappointed in one of the children's progress and asked the teacher whether she thought the child was slow. "It just floored me because of what this little girl had been through. I said I was just hoping that she made it through as a *human being* that year." The child's teacher was flexible enough to understand the complexity of the situation and adjust her priorities accordingly.

We turn our attention now to how teachers combine these facets of intrapersonal knowledge with their professional and interpersonal knowledge to structure the intellectual environment of their classrooms.

Structuring the
Intellectual Environment

6

While we are teaching we are learning.
Seneca, *Epistolae, VII, 8, A.D. 63-64*

Tom sagged into his armchair, loosened his damp collar, and wiped his glasses. "I feel like a rag," he said to Rosario, his student teacher, as she slid into one of the third-grade chairs and propped her elbows on the desktop. His eyes brightened as he added, "But did you see how hard the kids were thinking? Boy, were they working!"

"Were you always this good?" Rosario asked in a worried tone.

"No way! And tomorrow, when you work with the one group," Tom leaned forward to emphasize his point, "I want you to concentrate on only one thing, and that's whether the kids are able to help each other add or subtract words to their lead paragraph to make it more interesting."

"What's the difference now?" she persisted. "I mean, what's the difference between what you did today and what you did maybe ten years ago?"

Tom clasped his hands behind his head and looked out the window. He had taught various grades before being assigned his present class and he had been pursuing a master's degree in reading during part of the last

84

decade. "Ten years ago," he said, "I was very unhappy with how I was teaching. I liked the rapport I had with my students. I liked being with them, but I didn't like my lack of knowledge at all. So I decided to go where the emphasis was, at least in my mind. I figure that if kids can't read, they eventually can't do much in other subjects either. So I decided reading would be my focus and I knew I needed something more than I had. That's when I decided to go to graduate school."

Rosario's brow furrowed. "But weren't you a good teacher ten years ago?"

"Oh, I always got outstanding performance evaluations, if that's what you mean," Tom laughed. "I was doing activities that foster learning. I really let the kids read, I let them write, we did projects that were very open-ended, they talked to me, I talked to them, they read to me, I read to them. But there was very little structure to it because I just let them go with the activities. I probably needed to establish my own criteria a little bit more. I needed to let the kids establish more of their criteria too. I knew I was making connections for the kids, but I didn't have enough knowledge to know how to change. At times, I knew I wasn't giving them the correct kind of input because I wasn't seeing growth in the directions I wanted. So I knew that I needed to be doing something different."

Rosario looked away, trying to absorb what Tom was saying. "I never thought about teaching that way before," she said at last. "I thought that when I became a teacher, I'd be 'The Teacher.' I guess I never pictured myself in my own classroom as a teacher and a student at the same time."

"Oh! But you are!" said Tom. "You learn from the usual sources— conferences, workshops, books, colleagues, thinking—but you also learn a lot from watching kids."

"So what changed for you?"

Tom noted the anxiety in her tone of voice. He paused, trying not to overwhelm her.

"I found out, first of all, that the only way somebody's going to learn something is by doing it—doing it a lot and relating new experiences to their own experiences. I started to see learning as a continual process—for them and for me. You noticed that I had planned too much yesterday. The kids were done in. So I had enough sense to know to stop. I didn't push my lesson plan. We went back to it today and I got that excitement back again by asking the class how many of them had ever read the first two sentences of a book and then put it away because it was boring. Hands went up all

over the room. I said, 'We all love James and the Giant Peach. *Now let's see why.' Well, we read the first paragraph and it was obvious; it has an interesting introduction."*

Rosario laughed as she said, "Well, the kids sure weren't shy about telling you which books have interesting introductions and which ones are boring."

Tom smiled and nodded. "So when we wrote our model story, most of the time was spent on the lead sentences, getting them just right. I said to the kids before we started, 'I don't know what this story is going to say. This is your story. I will help you with it, but I don't know the way this is going to turn out. All I know is, anytime you want to change your mind, you go back to your outline, change it, add things, scratch things out that aren't fitting. You make it work.' And they did!"

"You're right," Rosario said. "The way the main characters met each other turned out to be different from the way the class originally thought on their outline. And I literally heard your voice when Samantha said to herself, 'Oh, this isn't going to fit. I'll just scratch this idea.' "

Tom started to laugh. "They never miss a trick," he agreed, "and you can't believe how much scratching things out appeals to this age level. But what's really great was that Sara had a true lead sentence. All year, she's started every writing piece with 'I like . . .' Today, she wrote, 'One day, the Hogan family woke up and thought it was a normal day.' It was so sophisticated I could hardly believe it! This was the most successful getting-it-started lesson I've ever done, and it had to have been because of the way I built it up. The kids were really thinking. It wasn't 'confusion thinking'; they were thinking about their story. It was a different kind of thinking. This was the best writing experience I've ever done with kids. And I don't think I'm as good at it yet as I can be. Something different might happen next year."

Teaching for Learning

Brophy (1989) has suggested that the following attributes would be evident in effective teaching: The teacher mediates student learning, academic activities promote active processing, the learning environment is supportive, and assessment methods reveal students' thinking. We have already seen how some exemplary teachers structure the physical and social environment in their classrooms to help students learn and how they work with parents to support learning within and beyond the classroom. In this chapter, we will examine the three remaining attributes Brophy has identified, attributes involving questions of how teachers view their role, how they view learning, and how they think about evaluating students' learning.

The terms *assessment, grading,* and *evaluation* are sometimes used interchangeably in schools. For the purpose of this book, I will use *evaluation* because the term implies judgment based on criteria that are valued. This term represents the direction in which these teachers are trying to move.

Learning to Think

Conversations with the exemplary teachers I've been referring to in earlier chapters make it clear that they put thinking at the center of the curriculum and that they select learning materials and experiences that help children think. If materials or books don't help students think, they don't use them. Instead, they look for other workable materials, make their own, or have students create them. Exemplary teachers often spend time searching for books at the public library, looking for help in the community or at conferences, or looking for teaching aids such as posters or brochures even when on vacation.

What appears to have happened is that most of these teachers began their career by reading and following the district's course of study guidelines. As they expanded their professional knowledge, became more skilled and secure in a particular grade level, recognized patterns across the curriculum, and began to know what to expect from students, they figured out ways to emphasize what is vital to children's understanding of concepts. Now, as experienced teachers, they focus on conceptual understanding, usually by selecting broad interdisciplinary themes as a vehicle for teaching concepts. A few teachers started their career using thematic teaching thanks to cooperating teachers or more experienced team partners; others eventually began using themes as a way to organize information to help students learn. The common thread is that they moved in the direction of a holistic curriculum.

My kids never ask, "Are we doing science now?" They'll say, "We're learning about trees." And when we're learning about trees, we're doing art lessons, we're rubbing tree bark, we're learning the parts of the tree, we're naming the kinds of trees, we're learning where they grow, what will make them grow best, what they're used for. . . .

Once these teachers have clarified concepts and goals in their own mind, they try to challenge the class by stretching students as far as they can without discouraging them. Simultaneously, the teachers support their high expectations by offering appropriate help and encouragement. But they are also challenging themselves. Over and over, I hear the comment, "I can't stand doing something the same way twice!" Usually, this kind of statement is quickly qualified in two ways: Repetition of lesson plans rarely works effectively because each group of students is different and the teachers themselves have developed their own love of learning, curiosity, and creativity to a point where they enjoy challenging themselves to find better or more interesting ways to design themes or lessons.

There is another important reason why these teachers try to find many ways to present key concepts. They know that what works for one child may not work for another, and they are willing to give a student the benefit of the doubt, especially if they know the child well:

You have to try more than once because kids may be having a bad day or because it's just not a time when they can think about that particular task.

The teachers are very aware that children develop at different rates and bring different experiences to each lesson:

I know I must build on prior knowledge. I lead them through things and I'm doing it better this year than last year. Teachers need to know that this doesn't just happen and that the kids don't just give you every line. It's how you pull, how you question, how you feed the beginning of a sentence so they finish it, how you show them the transitions, how you show them the connectors, and how much work that takes.

Finding out *what* individual children think and *how* they think is a huge task for teachers. They understand that their challenge is to connect and extend what students know. Their underlying assumption is that children construct knowledge much as a contractor constructs a house: Bricks are laid on a solid foundation and cemented together. When teachers structure the intellectual environment from a constructivist conception of learning, and when they focus on making the curriculum a thinking curriculum, there are two areas to which they pay close attention: having students apply knowledge to demonstrate understanding and helping children learn about learning.

Demonstrating Understanding

There are many ways that we understand and many levels of understanding for every individual. In education, two kinds of understanding are usually discussed. The one that is most familiar to me from my elementary school days is "instrumental understanding" (Skemp, 1978). Instrumental understanding tends to rely on memorization, allowing us to learn a rule and apply it to a given situation. For example, I learned that in dividing fractions, I had to invert and multiply to get the correct answer, but I had no clue why the rule worked. So if any part of the problem or context changed, I had few resources with which to check accuracy and I remained dependent on the teacher for help because I did not understand key mathematical concepts.

Another kind of understanding is "relational understanding" (Skemp, 1978) or "genuine understanding" (Gardner, 1991). Both are similar to "generative knowledge" (Resnick & Klopfer, 1989). The goal achieved is conceptual understanding, including the ability to apply learning and explain the how and why of a process. This knowledge or understanding also emphasizes continuity; in other words, students are making links or connections with existing knowledge to create new knowledge or understanding.

In the classroom, this means that teachers set up many opportunities for students to use different types of skills to apply what they have learned. These teachers have come to the same conclusion as Piaget (1948/1974) who observed in the title of his book that "to understand is to invent." They like to have students work on open-ended activities or projects that act as a culmination to a theme and that provide avenues for children to synthesize and apply in new ways what they have learned:

> The teacher must really watch kids and listen to what they're saying because that's where the teacher can become a facilitator

to help children apply what they know. Kids have notions of what they know, and they have this sense of vague directions sometimes that you can help them pinpoint. Then you can direct their ideas into something where you know they could really apply what you have just presented. So you've got to watch for their thought processes as they are learning and help guide them into how they can apply it.

There are many ways for teachers to check students' understanding. One technique that I liked to use, particularly in math, was to give the children a blank sheet of paper and ask them to create five problems to demonstrate the concept at hand. Groups of two then exchanged their problems and individually worked through them. When they finished, their partner checked their work. Not only did they have to understand the concepts to create the problems; they were sufficiently interested in the concepts to check their partner's work really carefully. Sometimes, one partner had to reteach the concept; occasionally, a problem was flawed and the children had to figure out why; and often, the students had to confer because each had solved the problem in a different way.

Getting at children's reasoning processes is very important to knowing how children think, and in effective classrooms, the most frequently asked question to uncover a line of reasoning is, "Why?" Reasoning extends the curiosity children exhibit from birth, but it also helps human beings make sense of their world. Anyone who has spent time with two- or three-year-olds knows that in their quest to make meaning of the strange new world around them, they ask "why?" so often that adults can become exasperated or exhausted by the process. Later, teachers reverse the process and make use of "why" questions to uncover students' thinking:

> When I took Math Their Way workshops, [the instructors] taught us little games and showed us how to explain to children what it is that they're doing so they understand. Now, when I go over that material in class and I call kids to go up to the board or up to the chart, I make them tell me why they're doing it. I'll say, "You put that number up there. Why did you put it there? What does it represent?" If they can verbalize it to me, then I know they understand it. Kids will do things, but they don't understand the meaning behind what they're doing. So if they have to extend the concept any further, they can't because they don't know why they're doing it.

Modeling is an important tool in assisting student understanding. As noted in the vignette at the beginning of this chapter, the teacher does not try to model what to think but, rather, how to think:

> The key is that you need to model for students what you want to see from them, and if you give them enough, they will take the ball and run with it. Of course you have students who will be doing this at a quicker rate than others, and once you have a core group of kids who can do it, you strategically formulate your groups by putting children who are leaders in a group of children who are just on the brink of getting it. They're going to work with one another and eventually, everybody's going to catch on and everybody's going to feel successful.

Part of modeling includes helping children learn how they think and how they learn. Modeling also includes letting children see or hear how teachers think through problems that arise. For example, one primary teacher frequently says, "Boys and girls, how can we work this out?" or "Do we have any strategies to help us here?" The following section illustrates how teachers deliberately structure the classroom to encourage and articulate positive ways of learning how to learn.

Learning About Learning

Learning about learning is often referred to as metacognition or "meta-learning" (Skemp, 1979). *Meta-learning* might loosely be described as figuring out how your brain learns, remembers information, and understands. Skemp (1979) describes it as "learning which takes place as a result of what is intentionally (and therefore) consciously being learnt. . . . A meta-learning which all too many persons have undergone at some time is that saying one doesn't understand, asking questions, [or] seeking an explanation [can result in] being made to look stupid, or told they should have paid proper attention" (pp. 262-263). In other words, both positive and negative learning about learning can occur. Whether subtle or blatant, verbal or nonverbal, teacher modeling is a powerful learning tool.

One of the most important ways to learn is to make connections with existing knowledge:

Kids are perceptive and they can be very keen observers. So I try
to have them make links when we read books and we do a lot of
reading. We relate what we read to experiences that they've had
or I've had and they'll say, "Oh, remember this?" or "It was just
like that." They're wonderful for doing that. But you need to show
them how to do it and then they'll do it.

Another teacher commented that she wants to avoid having students
think that learning is something you do for a test and then forget. She
specifically asks students, "How is this like something we've done before?" Eventually, as the class learns that making connections is expected,
they comment on the connections before being asked. They are engaged in
a mode of thinking that might not be evident to a casual observer.

Another way teachers demonstrate that they expect all students to think
deeply is to give children paper and have all of them jot down ideas or
comments in response to an open-ended question. The teacher waits and
then asks for responses from various students. Although this process
appears to slow down a lesson, the responses usually are more thoughtful.
Students get the message that everyone is expected to think, not just the
first person called to answer a question. In a trusting environment, the
teacher can say, "Did anyone approach this question from a different
position?"

A great deal of learning about learning in these classrooms focuses on
remembering and on making comments about the brain. One kindergarten
teacher is constantly looking for opportunities that allow her to capitalize
on spontaneous learning lessons. One day, in response to a child's comment, she said, "I'm going to make a mental note of that."

After a few minutes of conversation, an astute student interrupted the
class to exclaim, "But Mrs. Fahidy, you don't have any paper!"

"That's right," she replied seriously. "So where do you think I can put
my mental note?"

The class fell silent as they tried to solve this puzzle. Eventually, they
came up with the idea that the teacher was going to put the note in her brain.

"Good for you! That's exactly where mental notes are stored. Now, I
don't have a pencil either, so how do I put the note in my brain?"

As the exchange continued, the class came up with the idea that if you
want your brain to remember, you have to tell it what to remember. The
teacher used this insight to tell them that remembering is one way of using
their brain and that remembering takes practice, just like learning to play

baseball. Later in the year, the teacher asked the class how they learn. They said that "learning is using your brain" and they decided that in addition to storing things in their brain, they could pick out what they needed, they might have to put information back in their brain if it forgot something, and they had a brain database like their computer. The students were fascinated with the idea that their brains could move forward or backward in time while their bodies stood still.

A third-grade teacher gave each of her students a stenography pad to help them remember certain items that would eventually become automatic for them:

> The way I remember things is, I write them down and that works for me. So I tell the class that if there's something they want to remember, they should record it. This year, I've been experimenting with having the kids write certain things down that they will have for a reference. If they're reading on their own and they have difficulty with a word, I tell them to write it in their steno book. If they can't remember the meaning later, they look for the word in their story and then they've got the context for the word. It's really helped build new vocabulary. I gave them rules about "r" controlled vowels and long vowels and short vowels. They also made a big question mark for the *who, what, when, where, why,* and *how* when they're writing. And it's helped them; their writing's better.

When I taught fourth grade and higher, I often said to the class, "This is something I need you to put in your long-term memory bank because we are going to use it again in a couple of weeks. How would you like to remember it?" One particular fifth-grade class loved mnemonic devices and got very good at them. The point was, however, that in drawing their attention to the item and having them decide how it could be remembered, it was learned.

Of course, there are many opportunities and many different ways to draw children's attention to how they learn. Some comments that I have heard teachers say include the following: "Thinking is how your brain has fun." "Give me a minute to search my memory." "Let's stop and think about Darren's answer." "For five minutes, we're going to have quiet, independent thinking time." "Let's think this through." "Give your brain a workout. If it wants to do cartwheels, let it do cartwheels because you might see things from a different angle." Whatever the meta-learning process, children get the message quickly that they have within themselves a great deal of capacity to learn and remember and that they are expected to think deeply at school.

Establishing Dialogical Patterns: Listening and Speaking

Berman (1987) suggested that teachers who are interested in caring try to establish dialogical patterns that involve listening and telling. Just as the school can capitalize on children's gift of curiosity, so teachers can benefit from children's love of language and their desire to communicate. From birth, babies hear their parents talking to them and admiring their efforts to make sounds and, later, words. I first became aware of the magical sound of words for children when I taught first grade. Not only did they fall in love with specific words and repeat them endlessly as they worked, but they also loved rhyming words. Poetry and songs were enormously attractive to them and an easy way to build vocabulary.

Even though primary school children are still building their vocabulary, excellent teachers do not talk down to them by altering or simplifying the way they usually speak. Rather, the teachers spend considerable time concentrating on meaning and understanding, both verbal and nonverbal. One teacher had to step out of the classroom just as her class was ready to put away their activities for the morning. She quickly gave them instructions to tidy the room and sit down in front of her chair. When she returned a few minutes later, the class was quietly waiting for her. She was about to compliment them when she noticed that the activity centers were a mess. This class had learned the clean-up routines quickly and were unusually neat, so the teacher wondered why the habit had broken down in her absence: "Boys and girls," she said seriously, "I admit that I'm puzzled and annoyed that you came to the circle before finishing your task. Just because I'm not here to supervise is no excuse for shirking your responsibilities. I'm disappointed that I couldn't rely on you this time. We'll take the time now to tidy up properly, but I would like your assurance that this will not happen again."

Most of the students, having immediately picked up on her body language and tone of voice, avoided her eyes and squirmed miserably. Only one child looked at the teacher with an enraptured smile. The teacher had taught middle school long enough to know that older students know how to use smiling at any angry adult to exhibit insolent disregard or establish a protective facade, but she also knew that this young child's smile was genuine. Thinking that perhaps the child needed help in learning how to read body language, she said, "Jill, it's not appropriate to smile when I'm disciplining the class for unacceptable behavior."

"Oh, but Ms. Holton," the child sighed, "I just *love* hearing those big words!"

Excellent teachers also create or capitalize on every possible opportunity to have children talk and ask questions:

> You have to give them plenty of time to express themselves and really listen to them. Perhaps it's as they're coming in in the morning or as they are doing different activities or as they are talking in a group. You get to know a lot about them by listening to the kinds of things that are important to them and the way they express themselves.

This comment reminds us that listening is the corollary of speaking. In Western industrialized nations, people equate good listening with establishing eye contact. Lack of eye contact may be a cultural practice signifying respect for elders, but it may also indicate that some children simply don't follow expected patterns of any culture, making the teacher's observations essential:

> A lot of times, I'll have a kid who's not looking at me at all, but he knows every answer in the book. Harry is like that. He's always twirling around in his seat, but he'll tell you everything. He just doesn't listen by looking. Then there are other kids who are looking straight at you and have *no* idea what's happening. It's very hard to learn how to observe those kids and pick up on what they're doing.

This same teacher is also aware that students who love to talk can easily distract her attention away from her goal of providing opportunities for all children to talk:

> I try to make sure I'm giving feedback to every child or giving them an opportunity to talk sometime during the day. [Teachers]

tend to like the little quiet ones. I get worried I spend too much
time on the talkers.

In addition to being aware of developmental differences in students, these
teachers are also conscious of when some children will or will not speak. They
try to balance the amount of whole class instruction, small-group instruction,
and individual instruction. However, they like collaborative group work
because of the interaction time it allows students, and the observing and
listening time it offers teachers. Researchers believe that human interactions
assist in the kind of understanding that is so important to these teachers:

> An increasing number of studies suggest that learning activities
> embedded in social interaction engender more comprehensive
> understandings. Brown *et al.* (1989) contend that one of the
> benefits of collaborative learning is not simply the accumulation
> of the knowledge of individual members. Social interactions "give
> rise synergistically to insights and solutions that would not come
> about without them," that is, structures and meaning that do not
> exist in isolated or disconnected activity emerge via the social
> system. (Yinger & Hendricks-Lee, 1993, p. 109)

Another reason to structure the classroom so students have follow-up
time in groups is to allow for "kids teaching kids":

> Many times, one student will say to the other, "Oh, she means . . ."
> I've heard this over and over, especially when I've modeled
> something and they're working on it in cooperative groups. I love
> listening to their explanation of what I have just tried to get across;
> they're translating "teacher talk" into their own vernacular, their
> means of understanding. I love hearing the other child say, "Oh,
> now I understand!"

These teachers enjoy listening to and learning about their students'
thought processes and explanations, and they are frequently amused because students imitate the teacher's voice and patterns of speech. However,
a major reason to listen to children's thinking is to use the resulting
knowledge as a teaching tool:

> One of my favorite techniques is asking a child to write down what
> they're thinking or to explain their reasoning. Then I have the

children share their answers. I walk around and I observe while they're going through this process, so I know who has a clear understanding and who can concisely explain it. I call on those students first and then I call on those who were kind of in a gray area. By the time it's their turn, they've figured it out and they'll stand up and share something that wasn't written on their paper at all. During that period of time, they've learned from each other and they've gotten to the point where they understand.

Worth noting is that unintentional modeling by the teacher can be learned as quickly as intentional modeling. Also worth reiteration is that talking to children about their personal thoughts is important:

> My principal . . . embarrasses me when he calls me a "classroom wizard". . . . I don't have any magic. . . . If I have a secret, it is that I talk frequently to each of my students. I get to know all about them, their hopes, their fears, what they dream about, what kinds of pain they have known. . . . Knowing as much as I can about them and how they view their world helps me to think of ways to tap into their inner motivation. (Zehm & Kottler, 1993, pp. 111-112)

To know what children think, we must listen to them. To understand children, we must know what they think. And to encourage their dreams and help them bring meaning to their life, we must know their dreams. Teachers never know when something in the classroom may spark a dream in a child. But we need to have created an environment where children feel free to talk about their dreams, knowing the teacher will listen.

Evaluation: Observation, Judgment, Critique

By the late 1980s, researchers were beginning to codify certain teaching practices as "authentic instruction" and to establish standards or criteria to describe the kind of teaching that engages students' minds and helps them develop what Dewey (1933/1960) called "good habits of thinking." Newmann and Wehlage (1993) suggested five standards of authentic instruction: "higher-order thinking, depth of knowledge, connectedness to the world beyond the classroom, substantive conversation, and social support for student achievement" (p. 8).

Teachers who put thinking at the center of the curriculum, encourage questioning and student interaction, and provide opportunities for students to synthesize and apply knowledge to real-life situations quickly run into problems with the traditional evaluation process:

> Just the way we need to present things in many different ways at several different times, we need to evaluate in several different ways and at several different times because that's the only way we're going to get an accurate indication of what kids understand and what they can do.

Multiple choice tests, although they may be efficient for testing basic skills or facts, leave much to be desired if teachers are emphasizing careful thinking and reasoning:

> I was fascinated at looking at the kids' error patterns to find out why they were making mistakes. What were they thinking? Because then you know what you can do to help. That's why I don't like multiple choice tests; you don't know why the students selected the answer they did, so you can't help them.

These teachers are attempting to include open-ended classroom activities that will encourage their students to think and be creative, but many forms of evaluation are incongruent with this kind of instruction. Having choices (commensurate with responsibility and capacity) is appealing to children. Several teachers mentioned that even though multiple choice tests appear to offer choices, they somehow deny both respect and choice. They also frustrate teachers' efforts to know and understand a child:

> We're not really respecting children when we ask them to go through these motions because children can do a whole lot more than we give them credit for. I think we need to let them respond in writing and in talking and not just circle A, B, C, or D. It doesn't tell you anything. The thought behind what they're doing is what we need to look at.

Another teacher agrees, relating an incident that occurred after she had worked for months with her students to get them to give her the reasoning behind their math answers. As a teacher, she wanted to know their thought processes to decide how to intervene with appropriate assistance. By having students share their methods of solving problems with their peers, she was also trying to help them learn that there can be many ways of understanding and approaching problems. One of her students clearly appreciated the respect this teacher accorded her students as thinkers:

> One of my favorite student stories is about a little boy who really didn't care to write a lot down. We had been taking multiple choice math tests that the district required and in his self-evaluation, when he evaluated the tests, he wrote "I would much rather write one of *my* own answers than choose one of somebody else's!"

This child's comment reminds me of Todd. My first attempt to get first-grade students habituated to self-evaluation involved giving them small sheets of paper with a line for the student's name and three faces: a smiling face, a neutral face, and a sad face. I asked the children to circle the face representing how they felt about their work. One day, Todd brought me a piece of art in one hand and the self-evaluation sheet in the other. He fumbled for words, trying hard not to cry. When I finally realized that the three faces did not satisfy him, I asked him to draw a face by himself. Five minutes later, he presented me with a face almost entirely covered with an enormous smile full of teeth.

"My Mom's going to *love* this one!" he said, his eyes shining.

"Why is that?" I asked, wondering what his mother had to do with his self-evaluation.

" 'Cause it's her birthday and blue's her favorite color," he announced, proudly holding out his art for my admiration.

What he had done was to apply the lessons I had taught on how to mix white or black paint with colors to create tints and shades. His painting was a composition of beautiful blues. Thanks to Todd, I switched from my prepared self-evaluation faces to blank sheets of paper and learned that six-year-olds have great capacity for endless variations of satisfaction.

Teachers who espouse constructivist thinking have long been experimenting with multiple methods of assessment that more accurately reflect what their students are learning. They have several reasons for doing so: They want children to understand that learning requires a continuous cycle of goals, effort, and thoughtful appraisal; they want children to separate their work from their worth as an individual; and they want children to become independent learners capable of accurately critiquing their own and others' work. But whatever evaluation methods are selected, teachers' observation skills are critical:

> You're watching for body language, you're watching for facial expressions, watching how they relate to one another. When the children are working together, you can cruise around or just sit and observe what's going on and listen to their conversations. You can find out how much they've absorbed and how they're learning.

Several teachers "cruise" with a steno pad or Post-it Notes so that they can jot down what they have observed or remind themselves of something they need to reteach to a child. One teacher tries to keep a clipboard on which she notes the names of students who contribute to the class. She started recording her patterns of calling on students when she realized she had not heard from one child for three or four days. Another teacher likes to tape record her students reading or telling a story so she can follow their growth over time. She sometimes uses excerpts of the tapes during parent-teacher conferences.

All of these teachers have experimented with various uses of portfolios. Not only do portfolios help students and teachers see what and how students have learned, but it is much easier for parents to see children's development when they have concrete samples of work rather than when they are looking at an average of several test scores. Even when students have not written a wonderful story, for example, parents can look at preceding drafts and comprehend that their children have made progress over time. The portfolio puts the parent-teacher conference focus where it should be: on the child's work and growth. I liked keeping a calendar of achievements in each portfolio because unless children's breakthroughs are documented, they can easily be forgotten. The calendar noted the day on which I first saw a breakthrough, such as the accurate use of quotation marks, the application of base 10, or an attempt to indicate perspective in a piece of art.

These same teachers model reflection and deliberately structure a thinking and evaluation time for students at the end of an interdisciplinary theme or activity. When students can write, the teachers have them record their thinking on paper, not only as a way of making students conscious of their thoughts but also because the teachers value the comments as suggesting ways to improve their teaching and confirming or refuting their observations:

Over the years when we've done a major unit, I always put a reflection page at the end so that my kids have time to reflect on what they've learned. It's like a completion, you know. I ask the students to write down what they liked or didn't like, how they felt about it, what they learned, what kinds of things they were excited about, and how they are using what they've learned. I get a lot of information by reading their thoughts and it's very important for me as I plan future lessons. It's also interesting to me the way they put their thoughts down and the expressions that they use. It's feedback, so those reflections are very informative and really insightful.

The teachers are not asking their students to do something that they do not do themselves: self-evaluation and peer evaluation. One teacher started to tape record lessons to learn why she was having a problem:

I had a little girl who just wouldn't talk very much and so I taped myself to see what I was saying. How did she react? When did she ever talk? What did I say that caused her to talk more? You can't think about that while you're busy working with the child, so taping is helpful.

The teachers think a lot about their workday after school. This form of self-evaluation tends to rely on observation, and it requires honesty and a desire to improve. Following is a sample of the kinds of questions teachers ask themselves:

- What did the kids really enjoy?
- Why did they enjoy it?
- Did it accomplish the intended goal?
- How did I manage the room during that time?
- How were materials being used?
- Do I need more materials?
- How could the introduction to the lesson be improved?
- Did everybody get a chance to talk?
- Why did Kelly's group have trouble getting started?
- What could I do differently?
- How could I make that lesson better?
- Was the transition to the next activity smooth?

Peer evaluation for teachers often occurs in the form of conversations with colleagues. With children, peer evaluation is usually carefully structured and age appropriate. A third-grade teacher was able to get very positive results with her first attempt at peer evaluation:

> One of the most effective methods that I used last year was during a long-term project. There were built-in moments where the students were to critique each other. I modeled how to do that: The students discussed with each other what they really liked about a particular project, and something that they still wanted to know or something that was left out. So it was done in a very positive way. They sat in pairs and talked to each other and wrote it down as well. Now if I had critiqued the projects, which I have done in the past, I would have gotten a certain response to my suggestions. But the kids followed each other's suggestions explicitly. They really listened and they critiqued very well.

If students have experienced modeling in the primary grades, they are able by fourth grade to "help" the teacher create criteria against which their projects will be evaluated. Children (and their parents) appreciate knowing precisely what they ought to be working toward.

Teachers work five hours a day to help children understand what they are to learn, why they are learning it, how they learn, and how learning can be evaluated. Simultaneously, teachers are learning about children and learning how to improve their teaching. Done well, this is a monumental and complex task that requires students and teachers to be both teachers and learners.

Becoming an Exemplary Teacher
A Way of Thinking, A Way of Being

Such people are not made to order. They make themselves that way.

Corazon Aquino (in Senge, 1980, p. 359)

Becoming an Exemplary Teacher

In the Introduction, I posed three questions: What is an exemplary teacher? What does excellence look like in the classroom? And what do exemplary teachers do to reach students to help them learn? To begin to examine these questions, I proffered a model that included development of a triad of knowledge:

- Professional knowledge (subject matter, curricular and pedagogical knowledge)
- Interpersonal knowledge (human relationships with students, the educational community, and the local community)
- Intrapersonal knowledge (reflection, ethics, and dispositions)

The examples throughout have indicated how carefully and thoughtfully exemplary teachers structure the physical, social, and intellectual environment of their classrooms to encourage and support student learning. How well exemplary teachers accomplish this depends on their own development of professional, interpersonal, and intrapersonal knowledge. How quickly teachers develop and apply their knowledge toward improving the quality of teaching and learning may depend on varying personal and professional factors. How and when development occurs is not the focus of this book. Development may be uneven across this triad of knowledge, but I contend that development of all three forms of knowledge is necessary for becoming an exemplary teacher.

This model does not contradict studies on exemplary teachers; instead, it incorporates characteristics identified by earlier researchers. Further work may reveal that there are other forms or aspects of knowledge not presently included. The model does, however, provide a new way to think about teacher preparation, career-long professional development, and evaluation of teacher performance.

I suspect that teachers who have worked to develop their professional knowledge can be very strong teachers. But this form of knowledge must be merged with the development of interpersonal and intrapersonal knowledge, because all three forms appear to be crucial to becoming an exemplary teacher. Especially notable, but perhaps most abstract, is the development of intrapersonal knowledge:

- a disposition toward continuous learning
- increasingly refined use of reflection (good thinking and judgment)
- development of an ethic of care
- development of a work ethic

In short, becoming an exemplary teacher is an ongoing process of development: a way of thinking and a way of being.

A Way of Thinking

Taken as a whole, the disposition toward continuous learning and the disposition toward reflection represent a recognizable way of thinking. Related dispositions include curiosity, creativity, risk taking, problem finding and solving, responsibility, and flexibility. "What sets good thinkers apart . . . is their abiding tendencies to explore, inquire, seek clarity, take intellectual risks, and think critically and imaginatively" (Tishman, Jay, & Perkins, 1993, pp. 147-148). In other words, good thinkers have developed "thinking dispositions" (p. 148). However, interpersonal knowledge is also vital in an environment dependent on social interactions.

I envision a conception of teaching that incorporates a disposition toward reflection, a disposition toward continuous learning, and the development of interpersonal knowledge as intercreative thoughtmapping. *Inter* represents the social interaction and interdependence of learning within a community of teachers and learners. *Creative* reflects the idea of constructing knowledge or applying it in new or different ways, because each teacher and learner has different strengths and is building on a unique foundation of experiences. *Thought* denotes the centrality of thinking in the classroom, whereas *mapping* represents exploration and discovery, multiple and unknown possibilities and constructions, constant change and reconstruction, and an emphasis on thinking toward the future.

Dewey (1933/1960), Vygotsky (1978), and Piaget (1948/1974) each concluded that knowledge is actively constructed, but for years this idea did not seriously affect education. Buttressed by postpositivism, information process theory, cognitive research, and Bruner's extension of Vygotsky's work (e.g., Bruner & Garton, 1978; Bruner & Harste, 1987), the concept of knowledge as socially constructed has become more widely accepted. The concept requires reconsideration of familiar ways of knowing and knowledge acquisition.

Central to a theory of constructed knowledge is social interaction—the need to learn with others to see various approaches and alternatives to solutions, the idea of experts or "coaches" helping novices, and the belief that working together can help individuals extend their knowledge beyond what would have been possible alone.

An intercreative thoughtmapping conception of teaching values the idea that knowledge is interactively constructed, refined, and continuously reconstructed in a search for meaning and conceptual understanding. New information is assimilated or accommodated into an existing foundation or framework of knowledge; or it may be ignored or forgotten if learners make no connecting links to earlier experiences. Teachers and students alike become explorers seeking knowledge—knowledge that is not limited by statements such as, "You're too young for that!" or "We don't do that until Grade 5." Instead, the search for knowledge is encouraged with questions such as, "I wonder how we could figure that out?" or "How can we do that better?" Knowledge becomes a tool to assist thinking and is jointly constructed in a community that values thinking, speaking, listening, observation, and judgment.

This conception of teaching sees new understanding as a starting point: "No matter what our current beliefs, we can always go on to understand better, take our thoughts further, render our ideas more complex and adequate" (Duckworth, 1989, p. ix). Curiosity is a welcome starting point for framing a question or problem to think about and resolve or for producing new questions. The teacher helps students find and work through relevant problems that challenge but don't overwhelm them.

The constant blurring of boundaries between teaching and learning in these exemplary teachers' classrooms suggests to me that a teacher's disposition to learn is a vital cornerstone to becoming an exemplary teacher. An intercreative thoughtmapping conception of teaching envisions learning as a lifelong process of which formal schooling is but a part, albeit an important part that lays the foundation for mature, independent thinking and increasingly good judgment. Social interaction allows students to be both learners and teachers. Teachers, as adult learners, learn from and about the students. What the teacher knows about students influences what is taught, why it is taught, and how it is taught.

The Role of the Teacher

The role of the teacher and learner is critical. Teachers need to be willing to help students make connections between "real-life" experiences and school experiences. To do so, teachers must know their students well. Teachers also need to understand that there are multiple means to an end and that weighing and choosing from alternative perspectives or possible solutions stimulates thinking and teaches judgment. Teachers need a thorough grounding in what and how to observe. In addition, they need to know students well and exercise judgment concerning when and how to intervene in the best possible way for each student.

Aiming for conceptual understanding by students, exemplary teachers work to design a holistic curriculum. This demands a significant time commitment to select resources and create open-ended opportunities for inquiry. By observing and getting to know students, teachers help them learn more effectively and generate or extend knowledge. Constantly on the lookout for cues indicating student interest or incomplete understanding, teachers are more apt to depart from a plan of action if a new direction can further a child's learning.

Questions—indeed, all forms of knowing by communicating—take on a very important role. Teachers value questions and want both teachers and students to ask questions. Teachers question students and themselves to learn what and how they know. Students' knowledge or misconceptions direct the teachers' actions. Critical analysis and reflection of their own actions allow teachers to examine their practices, reasoning, and judgments so they can teach more effectively.

How we view knowledge acquisition is related to how we view intelligence. Exemplary teachers encourage intrinsic motivation in students by modeling the belief that problem finding and solving are ways to develop intelligence and ways to learn. Larkin and Chabay (1989) argued that "challenge, curiosity, and control work together to determine intrinsic motivation" (p. 160).

This conception of teaching requires teachers to understand clearly the concepts to be discovered and to design various learning opportunities that draw on, but also extend, the experiences of each student or particular class of students. This is a tall order, and it requires deep understanding of each student's knowledge and way of thinking. Also required is appropriate intervention to stimulate curiosity or help direct students toward further understanding of their thinking and learning processes.

A theory or philosophy can be understood only if it is examined and makes sense based on the knowledge one has. Although theories or beliefs are often implicitly learned by children, teachers must make an effort to examine their own beliefs and to understand how they affect children. "No amount of theory can affect children in schools except as it becomes a fundamental part of a teacher's thinking" (Duckworth, 1987, p. 84).

Teachers have an additional responsibility: to understand how children know and comprehend. To do this, teachers need to know students' strengths and experiences at school and outside of school. Thus, parents need to become part of the educative experience and another source for getting to know students. The wonderful opportunity of teaching is that teachers are in a position to improve teaching and learning by being both teachers and learners, observing both self and students, and contributing to an understanding of self and others.

"What you do about what you don't know is, in the final analysis, what determines what you will ultimately know" (Duckworth, 1987, p. 68). This conception of teaching encourages learners to inquire and to create knowledge by adding to, reorganizing, or applying what they know. "To be generative, knowledge must become the object of thought and interpretation, called upon over and over again as a way to link, interpret, and explain new information that students encounter" (Resnick & Klopfer, 1989, p. 209).

The same holds true for teachers as learners. To rephrase Duckworth's statement, how exemplary teachers model their disposition toward continuous learning and reflection profoundly affects what students ultimately think and know.

A Way of Being

One great legacy of exemplary teachers is to have taught students how to think so they can become independent learners. Perhaps exemplary teachers have realized that they cannot really teach unless their students want to learn. So, for them, cultivating a disposition toward continuous learning in their students is a fundamental goal—not only as a necessity for intrinsic motivation but also because these teachers' love of learning has so enriched their own lives that they want students to have opportunities to enjoy the same or a better quality of life.

A second great legacy that exemplary teachers leave with us, whether they teach us when we are young or old, inside a school or elsewhere along life's journey, is to have modeled an ethic of care and a work ethic. Imagining an enriched quality of life that does not include other persons is difficult. To be sure, how we think, what we think, and why we think in certain ways contributes to our uniqueness as individuals. But individuals do not grow and mature in isolation.

Many of our happiest memories involve other people and there is little of long-term value in our lives that is not in some way related to an ethic of care or a work ethic. For example, we are moved to help strangers during a disaster or to support family and friends during both happy and sad times. The care of others, the "footprints on our heart," helps us become what we are.

We also become what we are because of what we choose to work at and develop as habits. As a nation, we were proud when Cal Ripken, Jr. broke Lou Gehrig's record number of consecutive baseball games played. When interviewed by reporters, Ripken credited his achievement to the strong work ethic his father had taught him. He did not set out to break a baseball record—simply to work hard and do his best. In the same way, we are proud when our children walk across the stage for their high school diploma or are recognized for other achievements, because we know what it means to the recipient.

Gardner (1963/1981) observed that a recognizable attribute of a self-renewing individual is the motivation to do "something about which he cares deeply" (p. 17). When we find something about which we care deeply and pursue it, it has the capacity to give meaning to our life. Caring provides the impetus to make us work at a goal, to become competent, to do our best, and to persevere even in the face of setbacks. Exemplary teachers model this ethic and try to get to know their students so that they can help them find something about which they can care deeply and work to improve. Their hope is that some goal will eventually push students beyond themselves to benefit others.

To be an inspiration, a healer, a mature humane role model, and a "molder of dreams" (Doud, 1990), teachers need to develop in themselves "increasing conceptual complexity . . . and increasing interpersonal maturity as indicated by self-definition and self-other relations" (Hunt, Butler, Noy, & Rosser, 1978, p. 3). They also need to develop a "capacity for understanding and care . . . [a] shift from an egocentric through a societal to [a] universal moral perspective" (Gilligan, 1979, p. 442).

Ethics do not blossom in a vacuum. They take years of patient care and work to cultivate. Teachers have the potential to be a powerful influence in hundreds of children's lives during their career. A part of that influence was captured by Ginott (1972):

> As a teacher, I possess a tremendous power to make a child's life miserable or joyous. I can be a tool of torture or an instrument of inspiration. I can humiliate or humor, hurt or heal. In all situations, it is my response that decides whether a crisis will be escalated or de-escalated and a child humanized or de-humanized. (pp. 15-16)

"Kohlberg, as did Dewey, believed that the route to more mature values led by way of interpersonal growth. He proposed that if schools choose to educate for moral maturation, they must alter their teacher and student relationships" (Heath, 1994, p. 188). Knowing students in many different ways is vital to exemplary teachers. They need to know students to determine how far to challenge them without overwhelming them, to make connections between the curriculum and students' experiences and interests, to deepen students' conceptual understanding, to make better judgments, to discipline, and to figure out specific interventions for individuals. When students know and trust their teachers, their capacity to learn and be creative is enhanced.

There is always more to be developed and learned on the continuum of knowing, thinking, and becoming as it pertains to exemplary teaching. I have indicated that it is difficult for us as students or teachers to imagine what "better" or "excellent" can look like unless we see exemplars. I believe that if we are serious about wanting excellence in education, we need to find better ways to identify and learn from exemplary teachers. We also need to encourage and assist *all* teachers to undertake the journey toward becoming exemplary teachers so they can better teach and reach our nation's children.

References

Arlin, P. K. (1975). Cognitive development in adulthood: A fifth stage? *Developmental Psychology, 11*(5), 602-606.

Beck, L. G. (1994). *Reclaiming educational administration as a caring profession.* New York: Teachers College Press.

Belenky, M. F., Clinchy, B. M., Goldberg, N. R., & Tarule, J. M. (1986). *Women's ways of knowing: The development of self, voice, and mind.* New York: Basic Books.

Berliner, D. (1986). In pursuit of the expert pedagogue. *Educational Researcher, 15*(7), 5-13.

Berman, L. (1987). The teacher as decision maker. In F. Bolin & J. M. Falk (Eds.), *Teacher renewal: Professional issues, personal choices* (pp. 202-216). New York: Teachers College Press.

Berscheid, E. (1985). Interpersonal modes of knowing. In E. Eisner (Ed.), *Learning and teaching the ways of knowing: The eighty-fourth yearbook of the National Society for the Study of Education* (pp. 60-76). Chicago: University of Chicago Press.

Bolin, F. (1987). Teaching as a self-renewing vocation. In F. Bolin & J. M. Falk (Eds.), *Teacher renewal: Professional issues, personal choices* (pp. 217-230). New York: Teachers College Press.

Brophy, J. (1989). Conclusion: Toward a theory of teaching. In J. Brophy (Ed.), *Advances in research on teaching: Vol. 1. Teaching for meaningful understanding and self-regulated learning* (pp. 345-355). Greenwich, CT: JAI.

Bruner, J., & Garton, A. (1978). *Human growth and development.* Oxford: Clarendon.

Bruner, J., & Harste, H. (1987). *Making sense: The child's construction of the world.* London: Methuen.

Campbell, K. (1988). Adaptive strategies of experienced expert teachers: A grounded theory. *Dissertation Abstracts International, 50,* 03A. (University Microfilms No. AAC 8914070)

Carnegie Task Force on Teaching as a Profession. (1986). *A nation prepared: Teachers for the 21st century.* New York: Carnegie Forum on Education & the Economy.

Clark, C., & Peterson, P. (1986). Teachers' thought processes. In M. Wittrock (Ed.), *Handbook of research on teaching* (3rd ed., pp. 255-296). New York: Macmillan.

Cohn, M. (1992). How teachers perceive teaching: Change over two decades, 1964-1984. In A. Lieberman (Ed.), *The changing contexts of teaching: Ninety-first yearbook of the National Society for the Study of Education* (pp. 110-137). Chicago: University of Chicago Press.

Collinson, V. (1991). Unpublished raw data.

Collinson, V. (1994). *Teachers as learners: Exemplary teachers' perceptions of personal and professional renewal.* San Francisco: Austin & Winfield.

Dewey, J. (1938). *Experience and education.* New York: Macmillan.

Dewey, J. (1960). *How we think: A restatement of the relation of reflective thinking to the educative process.* Lexington, MA: D. C. Heath. (Original work published 1933)

Dewey, J. (1966). *Democracy and education.* New York: Macmillan. (Original work published 1916)

Doud, G. (1990). *Molder of dreams.* Colorado Springs, CO: Focus on the Family.

Duckworth, E. (1987). *"The having of wonderful ideas" and other essays on teaching and learning.* New York: Teachers College Press.

Duckworth, E. (1989). Foreword. In C. Fosnot, *Enquiring teachers, enquiring learners: A constructivist approach for teaching* (pp. ix-x). New York: Teachers College Press.

Easterly, J. (1983, October). *Perceptions of outstanding elementary teachers about themselves and their profession* (Tech. Rep. No. 1). Rochester, MI: Oakland University, School of Human & Educational Services.

Eisner, E. (Ed.). (1985). *Learning and teaching the ways of knowing: The eighty-fourth yearbook of the National Society for the Study of Education.* Chicago: University of Chicago Press.

Ennis, R. H. (1987). A taxonomy of critical thinking dispositions and abilities. In J. Baron & R. Sternberg (Eds.), *Teaching thinking skills: Theory and practice* (pp. 9-26). New York: W. H. Freeman.

Fenstermacher, G. (1990). Some moral considerations on teaching as a profession. In J. Goodlad, R. Soder, & K. Sirotnik (Eds.), *The moral dimensions of teaching* (pp. 130-151). San Francisco: Jossey-Bass.

Fine, R. (1985). *The meaning of love in human experience.* New York: John Wiley & Sons.

Fullan, M., & Hargreaves, A. (Eds.). (1992). *Teacher development and educational change.* London: Falmer.

Gardner, H. (1983). *Frames of mind: The theory of multiple intelligences.* New York: Basic Books.

Gardner, H. (1991). *The unschooled mind: How children think and how schools should teach.* New York: Basic Books.

Gardner, J. W. (1981). *Self-renewal: The individual and the innovative society.* New York: W. W. Norton. (Original work published 1963)

Gardner, J. W. (1990). *On leadership.* New York: Maxwell Macmillan International.

Gilligan, C. (1979). Woman's place in a man's life cycle. *Harvard Educational Review, 49*(4), 431-446.

Gilligan, C. (1982). *In a different voice: Psychological theory and women's development.* Cambridge, MA: Harvard University Press.

Ginott, H. G. (1972). *Teacher and child: A book for parents and teachers.* New York: Macmillan.

Glickman, C., Gordon, S., & Ross-Gordon, J. (1995). *Supervision of instruction: A developmental approach.* Boston: Allyn & Bacon.

Goodlad, J., Soder, R., & Sirotnik, K. (Eds.). (1990). *The moral dimensions of teaching.* San Francisco: Jossey-Bass.

Green, T. (1971). *The activities of teaching.* New York: McGraw-Hill.

Hargreaves, A. (1995). Development and desire: A postmodern perspective. In T. Guskey & M. Huberman (Eds.), *Professional development in education: New paradigms and practices* (pp. 9-34). New York: Teachers College Press.

Heath, D. H. (1980). Toward teaching as a self-renewing calling. In G. Hall, S. Hord, & G. Brown (Eds.), *Exploring issues in teacher education: Questions for future research* (pp. 291-306). Austin: University of Texas, Research & Development Center for Teacher Education.

Heath, D. H. (1986). Developing teachers, not just techniques. In K. Zumwalt (Ed.), *Improving teaching* (pp. 1-14). Alexandria, VA: Association for Supervision & Curriculum Development.

Heath, D. H. (1994). *Schools of hope: Developing mind and character in today's youth.* San Francisco: Jossey-Bass.

Holmes Group. (1986). *Tomorrow's teachers: A report of the Holmes Group.* East Lansing, MI: Author.

Holmes Group. (1990). *Tomorrow's schools: Principles for the design of professional development schools.* East Lansing, MI: Author.

Holmes Group. (1995). *Tomorrow's schools of education.* East Lansing, MI: Author.

Howey, K. (1985). Six major functions of staff development: An expanded imperative. *Journal of Teacher Education, 36*(1), 58-64.

Howey, K., & Strom, S. (1987). Teacher selection reconsidered. In M. Haberman & J. Backus (Eds.), *Advances in teacher education* (Vol. 1, pp. 3-30). Norwood, NJ: Ablex.

Hunt, D. E. (1971). *Matching models in education: The coordination of teaching methods with student characteristics.* Toronto: Ontario Institute for Studies in Education.

Hunt, D. E., Butler, L. F., Noy, J. E., & Rosser, M. E. (1978). *Assessing conceptual level by the paragraph completion method.* Toronto: Ontario Institute for Studies in Education.

Jackson, P. (1987). The future of teaching. In F. Bolin & J. M. Falk (Eds.), *Teacher renewal: Professional issues, personal choices* (pp. 43-158). New York: Teachers College Press.

Jackson, P. (1990). *Life in classrooms.* New York: Teachers College Press. (Original work published 1968)

Jackson, P., Boostrom, R., & Hansen, D. (1993). *The moral life of schools.* San Francisco: Jossey-Bass.

Johnson, W. R. (1987). Empowering practitioners: Holmes, Carnegie, and the lessons of history. *History of Education Quarterly, 27*(2), 221-240.

Joyce, B., & Showers, B. (1988). *Student achievement through staff development.* White Plains, NY: Longman.

Jung, C. (1954). The gifted child (R. F. C. Hull, Trans.). In H. Read, M. Fordham, & G. Adler (Eds.), *The collected works of C. G. Jung* (Vol. 17, pp. 134-145). London: Routledge & Kegan Paul.

Katz, L., & Raths, J. (1985). Dispositions as goals for teacher education. *Teaching & Teacher Education, 1*(4), 301-307.

Kramer, D. (1983). Post-formal operations? A need for further conceptualization. *Human Development, 26,* 91-105.

Labaree, D. F. (1995, May). *A disabling vision: Rhetoric and reality in "Tomorrow's schools of education."* Revised draft of a paper presented at the annual meeting of the American Educational Research Association, San Francisco.

Larkin, J., & Chabay, R. (1989). Research on teaching scientific thinking: Implications for computer-based instruction. In L. Resnick & L. Klopfer (Eds.), *Toward the thinking curriculum: Current cognitive re-*

search (pp. 150-172). Washington, DC: Association for Supervision & Curriculum Development.

Leithwood, K. (1990). The principal's role in teacher development. In B. Joyce (Ed.), *Changing school culture through staff development* (pp. 71-90). Washington, DC: Association for Supervision & Curriculum Development.

LeTendre, M. (1955, May 22). Thoughts on the business of life. *Forbes,* p. 302.

Lieberman, A., & Miller, L. (1990). The social realities of teaching. In A. Lieberman (Ed.), *Schools as collaborative cultures: Creating the future now* (pp. 148-159). London: Falmer.

Little, J. W. (1982). Norms of collegiality and experimentation: Workplace conditions of school success. *American Educational Research Journal, 19*(3), 325-340.

Lortie, D. (1975). *Schoolteacher: A sociological study.* Chicago: University of Chicago Press.

Malen, B. (1993). "Professionalizing" teaching by expanding teachers' roles. In S. Jacobson & R. Berne (Eds.), *Reforming education: The emerging systemic approach: The fourteenth annual yearbook of the American Education Finance Association* (pp. 43-65). Newbury Park, CA: Corwin.

McMahon, T. (1995, April). Quotable quotes. *Reader's Digest, 146*(876), 177.

McNergney, R., Lloyd, J., Mintz, S., & Moore, J. (1988). Training for pedagogical decision making. *Journal of Teacher Education, 39*(5), 37-43.

McShane, S. A. (1995, July 20). Board makes minor refinements to much-lauded art curriculum. *Grosse Pointe News,* p. 15A.

Mertz, R. (1987). *Teaching as learning: The personal dimensions of teacher growth.* Columbus: Ohio Department of Education.

Murphy, J. (1991). *Restructuring schools: Capturing and assessing the phenomena.* New York: Teachers College Press.

Newmann, F., & Wehlage, G. (1993). Five standards of authentic instruction. *Educational Leadership, 50*(7), 8-12.

Noddings, N. (1994). Foreword. In L. G. Beck, *Reclaiming educational administration as a caring profession* (pp. ix-x). New York: Teachers College Press.

O'Neil, J. (1992). Reinventing schools from scratch. *ASCD Update, 34*(9), 1-5

Penick, J., Yager, R., & Bonnstetter, R. (1986). Teachers make exemplary programs. *Educational Leadership, 44*(2), 14-20.

Perkins, D. N., Jay, E., & Tishman, S. (1993). Beyond abilities: A dispositional theory of thinking. *Merrill-Palmer Quarterly, 39*(1), 1-21.

Piaget, J. (1974). *To understand is to invent: The future of education.* New York: Viking. (Original work published 1948)

Pianta, R. (1993). Relationships influence success in early grades. *Commonwealth Center News, 6*(1), 1-2.

Pool, C., & Willis, S. (1993). Emotions and learning. *ASCD Update, 35*(5), 2.

Pope, A. (1968). An essay in criticism. In B. Evans (Ed.), *Dictionary of quotations* (p. 681). New York: Delacorte. (Original work published 1711)

Redl, F., & Wattenberg, W. (1959). *Mental hygiene in teaching* (2nd ed.). New York: Harcourt, Brace & World.

Reiman, A. J., & Thies-Sprinthall, L. (in press). *Supervision for teacher development.* White Plains, NY: Longman.

Rental, V. M. (1991). *Preparing clinical faculty: Research on teacher reasoning.* A paper prepared for the Urban Network to Improve Teacher Education (UNITE) Conference, Washington, DC.

Resnick, L., & Klopfer, L. (Eds.). (1989). *Toward the thinking curriculum: Current cognitive research.* Alexandria, VA: Association for Supervision & Curriculum Development.

Reynolds, M. (Ed.). (1989). *Knowledge base for the beginning teacher.* Elmsford, NY: Pergamon.

Rogers, C. (1969). Significant learning: In therapy and education. In L. F. Natalicio & C. F. Hereford (Eds.), *The teacher as a person* (pp. 99-115). Dubuque, IA: William C. Brown.

Schaps, E., & Solomon, D. (1990). Schools and classrooms as caring communities. *Educational Leadership, 48*(3), 38-42.

Schön, D. (1987). *Educating the reflective practitioner: Toward a new design for teaching and learning in the professions.* San Francisco: Jossey-Bass.

Seneca. (1906). In T. B. Harbottle (Ed.), *Dictionary of quotations (Classical)* (p. 87). London: Swan Sonnenschein.

Senge, P. M. (1990). *The fifth discipline: The art and practice of the learning organization.* New York: Doubleday/Currency.

Sergiovanni, T. (1992). *Moral leadership: Getting to the heart of school improvement.* San Francisco: Jossey-Bass.

Shanoski, L., & Hranitz, J. (1989, July 30-Aug. 2). *An analysis of characteristics of outstanding teachers and the criteria used by colleges and universities to select future teachers.* Paper presented at the Association of Teacher Educators Summer Workshop, Tacoma, WA.

Sherman, N. (1989). *The fabric of character: Aristotle's theory of virtue.* Oxford: Clarendon.

Shulman, L. (1986). Paradigms and research programs in the study of teaching: A contemporary perspective. In M. Wittrock (Ed.), *Handbook of research on teaching* (3rd ed., pp. 3-36). New York: Macmillan.

Simmons, J., & Schuette, M. K. (1988). Strengthening teachers' reflective decision making. *Journal of Staff Development, 9*(3), 18-26.

Skemp, R. R. (1978). Relational understanding and instrumental understanding. *Arithmetic Teacher, 26*(3), 9-15.

Skemp, R. R. (1979). *Intelligence, learning, and action: A foundation for theory and practice in education.* New York: John Wiley.

Sprinthall, N., & Thies-Sprinthall, L. (1983). The teacher as an adult learner: A cognitive-developmental view. In G. Griffin (Ed.), *Staff development: The eighty-second yearbook of the National Society for the Study of Education* (pp. 13-35). Chicago: University of Chicago Press.

Starratt, R. J. (1991). Building an ethical school: A theory for practice in educational leadership. *Educational Administration Quarterly, 27*(2) 185-202.

Sternberg, R. J., & Horvath, J. A. (1995). A prototype view of expert teaching. *Educational Researcher, 24*(6), 9-17.

Stone, I. (1987). A phenomenological study of significant life experiences of "Teachers of the Year." *Dissertation Abstracts International, 48,* 11A. (University Microfilms No. AAC 8801992)

Tishman, S., Jay, E., & Perkins, D. (1993). Teaching thinking dispositions: From transmission to enculturation. *Theory Into Practice, 32*(3), 147-153.

Van Schaack, H., & Glick, I. D. (1982, February). *A qualitative study of excellence in teaching and the search for excellence in teaching: An annotated bibliography.* Washington, DC: National Institute of Education, ERIC Clearinghouse on Teacher Education.

Vygotsky, L. (1978). *Mind in society: The development of higher psychological processes* (M. Cole, V. John-Steiner, S. Scribner, E. Souberman, Trans.). Cambridge, MA: Harvard University Press.

Waller, W. (1965). *The sociology of teaching.* New York: John Wiley & Sons.

Weisburd, S. (1987, November 7). The spark: Personal testimonies of creativity. *Science News, 132,* 298-300.

Westerhoff, J. (1987). The teacher as pilgrim. In F. Bolin & J. M. Falk (Eds.), *Teacher renewal: Professional issues, personal choices* (pp. 190-201). New York: Teachers College Press.

Willie, R., & Howey, K. (1980). Reflections on adult development: Implications for inservice teacher education. In W. R. Houston & R. Pankratz (Eds.), *Staff development and educational change* (pp. 25-51). Reston, VA: Association of Teacher Educators.

Yinger, R., & Hendricks-Lee, M. (1993). Working knowledge in teaching. In C. Day, J. Calderhead, & P. Denicolo (Eds.), *Research on teacher thinking: Understanding professional development* (pp. 100-123). London: Falmer.

Zehm, S., & Kottler, J. (1993). *On being a teacher: The human dimension.* Newbury Park, CA: Corwin.

Index